Contents

Training Theory
— for —
Martial Arts

TONY GUMMERSON

First published 1992 by
A & C Black (Publishers) Limited
35 Bedford Row, London WC1R 4JH

ISBN 0 7136 3400 6

A CIP catalogue record for this book is
available from the British Library.

Acknowledgements
Line drawings by Taurus Graphics and
Sonja Williams.

Typeset in Monophoto Joanna by
August Filmsetting, Haydock, St Helens.
Printed and bound in Great Britain by
Hollen Street Press Ltd of Slough.

Acknowledgements

The production of this book and the concepts and ideas which it contains have been influenced by all the students and coaches of the martial arts with whom I have had the pleasure to work. I am particularly indebted to Wilf Paish, British Athletic Federation National Coach, who has guided many athletes of various sporting disciplines to national, international and Olympic success. It was Wilf who nurtured my sporting career and created my personal desire to understand the training process.

I would also particularly like to thank the martial arts governing bodies with whom I have worked, and who have given me the opportunity to apply 'training theory' to their particular style. Their kindness, goodwill and support have been spurs to the production of this book.

'By failing to prepare you are preparing to fail.'
Abraham Lincoln
Former President of the United States of America

The coach needs to have an indepth knowledge and thorough understand-ing of his style. He must also have the ability to pass them on to others

Introduction

If martial arts instructors are asked, 'What are the three most important attributes a coach needs to be effective, they will probably answer:

1. a high level of personal technical excellence
2. a thorough understanding of the history, tradition and evolution of the style
3. an ability to understand and communicate with people.

No one could argue with these replies, yet one very important aspect is missing, namely planning. Without a carefully prepared, systematic and progressive programme of training, students will not learn skills and develop technical excellence in the most efficient manner.

The ability to coach well has often been described as an art. It requires sensitivity to identify the potential and commitment of students, and to help them realise their ambitions. However, what is not always realised is that each lesson is a vital part of an overall plan. The aim of any training programme should be to encourage each student to achieve his potential. Lessons are units which facilitate the overall developmental process. The following sections give coaches an insight into, and an understanding of, the planning process. These in turn will ensure that each student achieves his potential, no matter what the level of ability.

Throughout the book the student and the coach are referred to as 'he'. This should, of course, be taken to mean 'he or she' where appropriate.

Coaches teach students, not techniques! The underpinning theme of all martial arts is that through the training process the individual student develops personality and character. Any fighting skill, grading or competitive success obtained is of secondary importance

I

Coaching – art or science?

The role of the coach in the martial arts is different from that of coaches in many other sporting activities. Although the martial arts, like other sports, require coaches with good personal and communication skills, very few sports require coaches who have been committed practitioners for a considerable number of years. Time spent learning and refining a particular fighting style is necessary, since a martial arts coach needs to have a thorough understanding of a particular technique in order to pass on his knowledge. However, it is now widely acknowledged that even if a martial arts coach has a high degree of personal, technical and practical ability, he does not necessarily have the ability to communicate this to others. In fact the most skilful practitioners are those who have a high degree of natural ability which has been channelled into a chosen style. Because they have a natural aptitude they often lack an understanding of sportsmen who are not as gifted, committed, enthusiastic and dedicated as they are, or who have difficulty in overcoming problems experienced in training. Years of training in any of the many fighting styles do not necessarily give the ability, or the experience, to coach others.

The evolution of most fighting styles has been quite effective, despite an apparent lack of organised development. In the last 20 years there has been a revolution not just in numbers of participants in the martial arts in general, but also in the analysis of techniques, in an attempt to improve standards of performance at all levels. There is in the martial arts something of a dilemma. The term 'martial arts' indicates an element of creativity and subjectivity—there is an implication that the practitioner is able to express his own personal interpretation of a technique within the constraints of physique, ability and the tradition of the style. A recognisable example is the practice of katas, patterns and forms. Most certainly there is a theme of quality of movement common to all martial arts. Perhaps personal performance and the evaluation of quality of movement are the art. Tradition, philosophy and art are closely interwoven in all styles, and will continue to be. This strong link with the origin and evolution of various styles tends to create mistrust in the application of a more scientific approach to training, grading and competition.

It might be argued that many of the responsibilities and duties of the coach are an art. Being able to motivate students is not a precise and rigid activity, since much depends on the coach's sensitivity in assessing the personality, attitude, commitment and ability of each student in his class. Once he has this information he can decide what is the appropriate way to get the best out of each student, by identifying strengths and weaknesses and developing a suitable coaching style. Similarly, the coach has to be able to evaluate each student's progress in class, grading and competition—once again a very subjective task. How does a coach 'measure' whether a student is training too hard, or not hard enough; becoming frustrated; becoming bored; or falling ill? These are all qualitative assessments and may be regarded as part of the 'art' of coaching (fig. 1).

Physical activities of all kinds give 'sports scientists' an opportunity to apply scientific principles to both preparation and performance in competitive situations. Sports science has developed along various lines: biomechanics, psychology, nutrition, physiology and sports medicine. The desire for ever-improving standards of performance means that both athletes and coaches are turning more and more frequently to sports scientists for help.

Though the present high standards of performance in all styles are mainly due to traditional methods of instruction and preparation, a more effective approach could be taken if the relevant areas of sports science were investigated and, where appropriate, adopted. The martial arts have their success firmly rooted in the past, but any future achievements will be based on willingness to adapt to increased knowledge in the area of sports science. Such knowledge will not only ensure the evolution of fighting styles at the highest technical level, but will also be of benefit to every student, no matter what his level of proficiency and commitment.

Many 'modern' concepts of 'coaching theory' have formed an integral aspect of martial arts for years. Most coaches seem able to create effective and efficient training programmes without being aware of it. Not all coaches are aware, however, of the elements of good practice in the

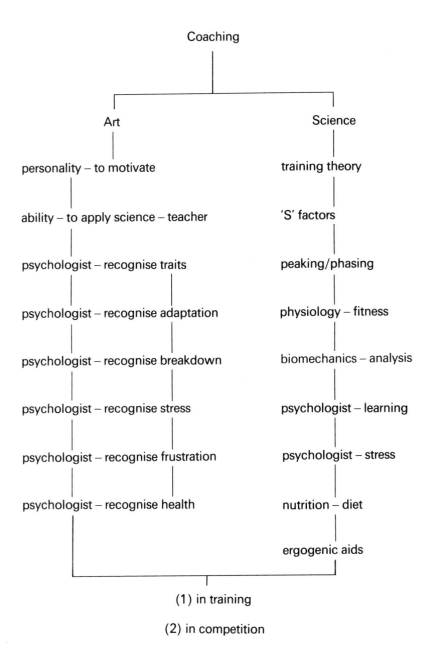

Fig. 1 Coaching is a complex mix of art and science. The coach has to blend the various elements to suit each student

development of an individual student's standard of performance. When assessing the quality of overall performance, several factors have to be taken into account (fig. 2).

The most important element is the student. His level of commitment, state of health, ability and potential must be considered at all stages of development. There is a need for the coach to assess a student's performance at key stages in order to establish systematic and progressive improvement. This is invaluable for developing a 'student-specific' train-

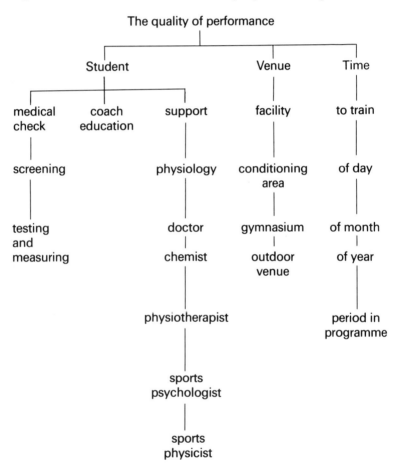

Fig. 2 The quality of performance involves many factors. The degree to which these are present or utilised will affect a student's rate of learning, and ultimately his level of achievement

ing programme and identifying problems as training progresses and for modifying the work schedule accordingly. The coach must possess sufficient knowledge to coach his students to the levels to which they aspire. Coach and student must work as a team to produce improvement, but they must also have assistance, where appropriate, from medical and sports scientists to ensure continued and systematic development. However, the best efforts are of little value without an adequate venue for training, competition and ancilliary activities. Standards of performance

Knowing how the body responds to certain types of training allows the coach to design work programmes to bring about specific adaptation

are directly related to the amount of time invested in preparation. The total amount of time spent is a critical factor, as are the part of the day available for training and the period that the student is in with respect to both long-term and short-term preparation. Where female students are concerned, the effects of the menstrual cycle must also be considered.

Although it might be argued that a scientific approach to preparation is the key to improved performance, the role of the coach should not be undervalued. He must make himself familiar with current training theory, but must also possess the sensitivity to assess its application to each student so that full potential can be achieved. The correct mix of these elements creates the best possible relationship between coach and athlete, and produces optimum performance. They have been termed the 'S' factors in an attempt to simplify a potentially difficult topic. Each coach will have his own view about the essential elements of performance. However, the 'S' factors are normally identified as:

- strength
- speed
- stamina
- suppleness
- skill
- (p)sychology.

Not only should the contribution of each of the 'S' factors be considered, but also how they can be combined to produce an ideal balance for each style and student. Modern notions of 'training theory' or 'periodisation of training' are jargon for the construction of training programmes encompassing all the 'S' factors, and for the underlying sports science. Each of the following chapters makes suggestions about training, grading and competition. If the coach applies the principles in this book, he will be able to construct more efficient programmes.

2

General principles

The human body is very adaptable to lifestyle. It is able to modify the function of the various systems to meet the demands placed on them exactly. When we are sitting quietly, our energy requirements are low. Consequently energy production and heart and respiration rates are low. However, if we are involved in very strenuous activity, heart and respiration rates rise dramatically, providing a level of energy that exactly meets our needs. Obviously the manner in which any individual responds to extreme workloads depends on the condition and coordination of the body systems and their ability to meet these demands. Any exercise carried out conscientiously and systematically over a period of weeks, months or even years will bring about physical changes within these systems. Improvements in performance in any physical activity will be directly related to them. By systematically exposing the various body systems to specific types of training, they gradually become more efficient in responding to workloads.

The coach must be constantly aware of the physical adaptation taking place within the student as a result of training. This adaptation is the main aim of all training, and must be uppermost in the coach's mind during the design and application of work schedules. Any physical adaptation must be brought about by design, not chance. And, perhaps more importantly, any adaptation should be planned specifically for the particular student and martial art—any other might be detrimental to overall performance. The coach should have a clear understanding of the effects of physical activity on the major physiological systems. Knowing how the body responds to specific types of training will allow the coach to design work schedules to bring about specific developments in body systems.

Training load and adaptation

Any adaptation to training is the direct result of the loading of a particular system. The process of loading is known as 'stressing'. When a stress is experienced over a long period there is adaptation, and as a result the body system will be more efficient than before. There are several key elements to consider.

All physiological adaptation is specific to the stress

If a student is involved in speed training he will become faster. He will not become more flexible, stronger, or develop endurance. Any training adaptation is highly specific to the way in which it is used. Quite simply, it is the *exact* function of the heart, lungs, muscles, nerves and joints, or their co-ordinated action, which adapts. The degree of adaptation will be proportional to the training load. Within certain limitations (which will be discussed later), the harder you work, the more your body adapts to that type of work.

All adaptation takes place in the recovery

It is often not fully appreciated that adaptation to physical activity occurs in the recovery period. The various body systems adapt to the training

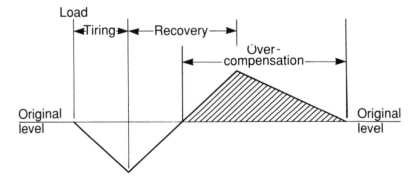

Fig. 3 The Theory of Overcompensation
During strenuous physical activity, exercise uses up stores of energy, builds up waste products and stresses body tissue. In the recovery phase the stores of energy will be overfilled and waste products removed. Body tissues will be strengthened and made more efficient

load by becoming more efficient or stronger, so that next time they are exposed to the same intensity of work they can cope with it far more easily, with less stress. It follows that by being able to handle a given workload more easily, a body system can deal with even greater intensities of work. This physical adaptation to training is referred to as the 'Theory of Overcompensation' (fig.3).

All students have an habitual level of fitness to cope with the stresses of training for their specific style. As the activities progress during a lesson, students become increasingly tired. The sensation of feeling tired is usually referred to as 'fatigue'.

Fatigue in itself is not quite as simple as it may seem. It can occur as the result of several factors.

The steady depletion of stores of energy throughout the body

The body has only a limited supply of energy, which is stored in the form of glycogen primarily in the muscles and liver. Large stores of fat are distributed throughout the body. However, the demands of martial arts training tend to identify glycogen as a main source of energy. The longer the lesson, or the more intensive the work, the more rapidly glycogen is used up. Many martial arts lessons are too long. An hour is enough, for most students, though many lessons last one-and-a-half to two hours, or even longer. The quality of training is affected by rapidly reducing levels of energy.

The build-up of waste products

The human body produces energy best when there is an abundance of oxygen in the bloodstream. This is usually brought about by aerobic work. When there is a ready supply of oxygen and nutrients, the waste products produced by physical activity are mainly carbon dioxide and water. The body's waste-removal systems are quite efficient in transporting these substances away from active body tissues. However, when there is an insufficient supply of oxygen to meet work requirements, energy is produced without it. This is known as anaerobic work. Anaerobic energy produces a waste product, lactic acid, which tends to build up in active tissues mainly because the body is not very efficient at removing it. The problem is that the lactic acid builds up faster than it is removed.

Eventually so much is present that it all but stops the production of energy. As training, grading or competition continues, the build-up of lactic acid dramatically reduces the work rate and the efficiency and quality of movement. It is also associated with the stiffness that accompanies intensive work.

The physical breakdown of tissue in individual organs

During any physical activity there is a need to repair tissue that has been damaged. The degree of damage will be proportional to the intensity and

Techniques will develop in exactly the way they are practised

duration of the activity. As training, grading or competition continues, a gradual accumulation of minute tissue fragments takes place. It may be that the gradual build-up brings about an ever-decreasing ability to produce energy or work. In extreme cases the damage is so severe that it forms an injury. The pain and damage prevent any further activity, and qualified medical attention is necessary. The amount of time tissue needs to repair depends entirely on the amount of damage.

The Theory of Overcompensation is directly related to the recovery process. After strenuous physical activity the body has several problems to resolve. Firstly, all the energy used has to be replaced. This is facilitated by resolving the second problem, removing all the waste products and tissue fragments which have built up. Blood supplies can then flow freely into affected areas, speeding up the transportation of nutrients and oxygen, while at the same time increasing the rate of waste removal. When all the debris has been removed and there is a ready supply of all the materials required, the body can begin to repair affected tissues.

With the replenishment of energy and the repair of tissues, the body demonstrates what is known as the 'Can't Cope Theory'. Since the body was not able to meet the demands of physical activity easily last time, rapidly using up energy and breaking down tissue, with a resulting build-up of waste, it attempts to make sure that the same thing does not happen again. This can be seen in fractures of the arms or legs. At the site of the injury more bone is laid down, producing a characteristic 'lump'. The body works on the principle that if a bone was not strong enough to cope with loads before, it will be in the future! Energy stores are overfilled, tissues are strengthened and the body's transport system is improved. Obviously it takes time for these processes to be completed. It might be hours or days, depending on the amount of repair and replenishment required. When designing training schedules, the coach must be aware of the physiological effects of training and recovery, and of the Theory of Overcompensation.

3

Training considerations

There are several important factors which can influence the effects of training on students, whatever martial art is practised.

Specificity

Training must be *specific to the requirements of the style or particular element of performance*. If a martial art or a particular technique within it requires mobility, training must include mobility activities. In addition, if a style or technique requires specific mobility in a particular joint or group of joints, the relevant part of the body must be isolated and developed. There is no point in encouraging students to develop strength, if mobility is what is required. Until specific mobility is achieved, the technical quality of movement will be severely restricted.

An aspect of training which the coach must take on board, although it might seem a little out of place, is that the learning of skills is very similar to the development of other physical attributes, such as speed, strength, suppleness and stamina. For example, if a technique is practised at speed, then it will be possible to perform it at speed when required. If, on the other hand, a technique is practised slowly, technical excellence and competence will be facilitated only when it is performed slowly. The manner in which techniques are practised *exactly* influences the way they develop!

Overload

To develop speed, strength, suppleness, stamina or skill, the specific parts of the body involved must be identified and worked in the required manner. However, if the work can be performed easily, it is within the ability of that particular system to cope adequately and no adaptation will occur. Obviously, if a student only ever kicks to mid section, technically excellent though it may be, it will not improve his hip mobility so that he can perform a roundhouse kick to the head. The student can only improve his hip mobility to do this by utilising joint isolation exercises on the hips, specific for such a kick, and by practising roundhouse kicks to head height. If any of the body systems are used within the normal demands of daily life or training, no adaptation will take place.

Any preparation for a particular martial art or technique must work each student generally, and the appropriate body systems particularly, at least to the level required for training, grading or competition. With some of the 'softer' styles and their essential philosophies, the idea of overload might seem out of place. However, if muscles, joints and connective tissues are not stressed in training to the levels to which they might be subjected, there will be a high risk of injury, simply because they will not have adapted to handle loads.

Intensity

The Theory of Overload suggests that body systems should be subjected to loads greater than normal, so that they can become stronger or more efficient. But what is the correct intensity of work to bring about these desirable changes? Any training load must be 'personalised', directly related to the individual student's existing levels of fitness and the requirements of the style or technique. Obviously, outside the normal physical demands of an individual's lifestyle training, grading and competition are going to place increased loadings on the student. It is these additional stresses over and above those of a normal daily life which will bring about any adaptation. Students with higher fitness levels will need more demanding training programmes to bring about improvement. No matter what the student's fitness level, however, the intensity of training must not be so great that recovery and adaptation cannot take place before the next training session. The coach must be aware that 'class training' is not an effective way of ensuring individual development. The warm-up for an élite performer might be more demanding than the entire training period for a less able student. In 'class training', every student is performing the same activity or technique, so it has to aim for the middle ground. This means that élite students will not be stressed enough, while less able students will be over-stressed and will not recover by the next session. In either instance the optimum conditions for adaptation will not occur, and no one will obtain the best possible benefit from the lesson.

Progression

Linked to both overload and intensity is the rate of progression of the training load. As the body and its specific systems begin to adapt to a training load, then and only then should the load be increased. Progression in the training load is in steps and only occurs when tissues have adapted to the previous level of work. Too rapid a progression, when tissues have not fully adapted, or too great an increase in work loads, can create the potential for serious injury. It takes time for tissues to become physically stronger or more efficient. In many cases at least six weeks should be allowed before there will be measurable improvements. Coaches and students must realise that there is no 'magic programme' which will bring about adaptation. Any benefits from training will be long-term, but enthusiasm to progress too rapidly must be tempered with caution and a little common sense. Any increases in training load must be systematic and gradual.

Frequency

More is not always better. As with overload, intensity and progression, the frequency of training must match the ability of the student. As a rule of thumb, the frequency of training must be directly related to the fitness of the student. By and large, the fitter the student, the faster he recovers from the effects of training. He will therefore be ready for the next lesson sooner if he is fit. The less-able student must be subjected to a much lower work rate if he is to recover within the same timescale. This is very important to bear in mind when preparing lessons for students of all abilities, who train together on a regular basis two or three times a week. Should the coach wish to 'over-stress' a student, to push him to his limit, the student may require a longer period than normal to recover. The coach must be aware of this when he takes the next lesson.

Any conscientious martial artist realises that in order to gain the best possible benefit from training, he must practise regularly. Many students fail to achieve their potential because they do not train on a regular basis. It is not always the fault of the coach, or lack of specialist facilities, which hinders progress; sometimes the problem is a lack of commitment and application on the part of the student.

Duration

As with overload, progression, intensity and frequency, the duration or intensity of a lesson will affect students in different ways, depending on the fitness of each student. The more able students might be able to cope with a lesson of two hours duration, while the less able might be struggling after an hour. The fitness, age, sex, and potential of a student will markedly affect his ability to endure training. Two-hour lessons are far too long for the majority of martial artists, although they are accepted practice. An hour is long enough for most students.

Recovery

All the adaptive processes take place in the recovery phase or rest between training periods. For the various body systems to fully 'over-compensate', they must be given adequate time to do so. Overtraining or insufficient recovery between work periods reduces adaptation, increases the risk of injury and, in extreme cases, can cause illness. There has to be a balance between the intensity, frequency and duration of training and recovery. In a well-managed situation the best possible benefits from training can be achieved.

Reversibility

'If you don't use it, you lose it!' This is very important to bear in mind. Any benefits which a student gains from months, or even years of train-ing are not permanent. If there is a long lay-off from training, there will be a slow deterioration in general and specific fitness. If the lay-off period is long enough, a student can even revert to the level of fitness that he had before he started training. Thankfully this is not entirely true when it comes to skills. However, any level of performance is not permanent;

once it has been attained it must be at least maintained, otherwise a slow deterioration will occur.

Ability

Each student is born with innate abilities and varying potential for developing speed, strength, stamina, suppleness, skill and the ideal personality for their style. With carefully designed training programmes, each student will be able to achieve his personal potential. The coach's responsibility is to ensure that lessons meet the personal requirements of each and every student. The coach's responsibility is to devise and organise lessons to cater for the needs of the student; for too long it has been assumed that the student must meet the demands of the lesson. All lessons must be student-based, not style-based. Put simply, coaches must teach students, with all their personal strengths and weaknesses, and not just techniques. All too often coaches think that they must teach this or that technique in a lesson, and that a student must attain a given level of expertise. They regard failure on the part of a student to meet their expectations as the sole responsibility of the student. What is never considered is that the coach might have got it wrong. This is not entirely surprising given that there are very few, if any, other activities which attempt to cater for the needs of children and 'mature' students, males and females, the gifted and the ungifted, competitive or non-competitive, committed or uncommitted, or any other variable that can be identified, *all in one class*. The martial arts coach has a difficult problem to resolve in ensuring that each student in a class achieves exactly what he is capable of. However, a coach should not be daunted by the task. With careful planning he can present the martial arts as a sport—possibly the only one—which can cater for all its participants equally. The diversity of talents and abilities among martial arts students must not be seen as a potential weakness, but *as its strength*. What other sports and physical activities cater for such a wide range of abilities and aspirations?

4

Physiological considerations

The title of this section might seem daunting to the committed coach. However, it need not be. The Theory of Overcompensation has already been discussed in Chapter 3. This is the ability of the body, or any of its constituent systems, not only to adapt to the demands of training, but to 'over-adapt', bringing about an increase in strength or efficiency (fig.3). In planning a long-term programme of training, the coach must be aware of all of the variables which can affect the rate of recovery and overcompensation. He must bear in mind that recovery and its associated benefits is very much down to each student. However, there is one question that applies to all students. After an initial lesson, when should the next work period take place, that is, how much rest should there be between training units? Unfortunately there is no easy answer. In the short term there is an obvious point when the next lesson or training unit should take place, the peak of 'overcompensation'. If this notion is accepted, the overall performance of a student will progress in steps (fig.4). The importance of the correct timing of lessons can be seen in fig.5. Too much recovery between lessons or irregular training will result in little, if any, improvement. However, it would be simplistic to think that performance always progresses by the same increments. As a student approaches his potential, the performance increments decrease. The coach must also accept the 'human factor'; that is, even with the best possible lesson planning and application on the part of the student, intended improvements are sometimes not achieved.

How, then, does a coach identify the correct rest or recovery between training periods? In order to understand, we have to go back to the 'General Adaptation to Stress Theory'. Usually known as the G.A.S. Theory, this was first put forward in 1954 by Hans Selyle (fig.6). Selyle identified the fact that all athletes, no matter what their sport or activity, achieve the best possible rate of improvement if they are stressed or

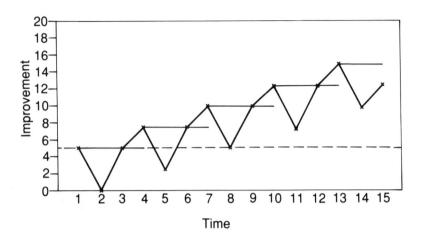

Fig. 4 Training progression
The ideal point in the recovery process for the next training session is during the period of overcompensation. If training coincides with this point on a regular basis, a student will improve in a systematic and progressive fashion

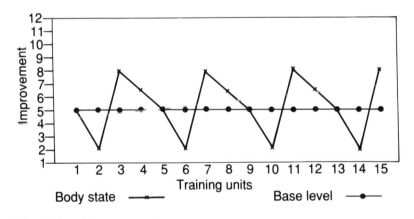

Fig. 5 No training progression
With too much rest between lessons, or irregular training, the benefits of the period of overcompensation are lost. There is a resulting lack of progress in performance—if there is any discernible improvement at all

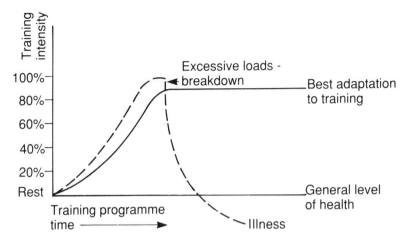

Fig. 6 General adaptation to stress
The body adapts to the demands of training if it is stressed to approximately 90 per cent of maximum

worked to 90 per cent of their potential. At first sight this may seem to contradict the Theory of Overcompensation, but actually it is not the case. In order to 'overload' a system or the entire body, there has to be a corresponding period of recovery or rest for tissue and energy stores to 'over-recover'. During a period of, say, a week, there will be possibly three intensive training sessions where a student is pushed to 100 per cent of his potential or even more. However there are also four days of little or no activity, which will bring down the 'overall' average of physical activity in the seven days of the week to 90 per cent. This figure is exactly in line with Selyle's theory.

Selyle did not suggest that all training sessions should stress a student to 90 per cent of his potential, whatever that might be, but rather that in a given period of time – a week, a month or a year – the overall loading of work and recovery should be 90 per cent. The way in which Selyle suggested that this might be brought about is shown in fig.7. There are only two variables for a student in a lesson: the intensity of the training, and the duration of the lesson. In fig.7, the student trains for a particular style on Monday, Wednesday and Friday, or three times a week. On these days the student is working to 100 per cent of his potential, or even more. However, depending on his level of fitness or commitment, the

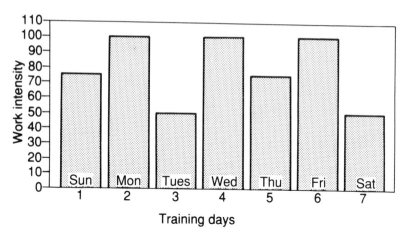

Fig. 7 The optimum training load
The G.A.S. Theory identified an optimal training load of 90 per cent. This can be achieved by balancing days of intensive training with less stressful activity

student might choose to rest or work on strength, suppleness, speed or stamina on his non-training days. The student is *not* stressing the *same* system on consecutive days, and therefore the *overall* level of stress to the body is 90 per cent. Fig.7 indicates how a balance of intensity and duration of work can meet both the demands of the Theory of Overcompensation and Selyle's General Adaptation to Stress Theory by achieving an optimum 90 per cent level during a seven-day training period.

Monday is an intensive training day, with loads of over 100 per cent, but with a corresponding lack of volume of work, perhaps a technique-specific day. Tuesday is characterised by rest or recovery, or by working a completely different body system, such as mobility or endurance. Wednesday is another intensive technical day, followed by another rest, recovery or training day with a different emphasis on Thursday. Friday is an intensive technical training day. It is followed by an 'easy' Saturday and an even easier Sunday. By working specific body systems on alternate days, sufficient recovery is ensured.

In reality it might work like this:
- Monday: specific martial art training (skill)
- Tuesday: gentle jog (stamina)

- *Wednesday*: specific martial art training (skill)
- *Thursday*: mobility work (suppleness)
- *Friday*: specific martial art training (skill)
- *Saturday*: strength training (strength)
- *Sunday*: rest or gentle exercise.

On consecutive days no system is stressed in this programme, thereby allowing full recovery. Although a student may train every day, as long as he does not work the same body system on consecutive days he will create optimum conditions for adaptation. Classically, Body-Builders work their arms on Monday; abdominals on Tuesday; legs on Wednesday; arms on Thursday; abdominals on Friday, and legs again on Saturday. In this way they do not work the same muscle group or body system on consecutive days. On Monday they isolate all training on the arms. On Tuesday, while their arms are recovering, they work the abdominal muscles. On Wednesday, when the arms have almost recovered and the abdominals are well on their way to recovery, the legs are isolated. On Thursday the fully recovered and adapted arms are worked once again. On Friday the abdominals are exercised specifically again, and by Saturday the legs are fully recovered for yet another specific training session. Sunday is a day of complete rest, or a day of 'gentle' exercise or training. In this way the best possible combination of training, recovery and adaptation is achieved.

There is, however, a very important aspect of the Theory of Overcompensation to bear in mind. If the total average stress in a given period is over 90 per cent, 'negative health' becomes a possibility. A careful balance of training load and recovery is the key to optimum adaptation. If the load is too high or the recovery too short, or if there is a combination of the two, there will be regression rather than progression in the various body systems.

When the terms 'training load' or 'stress' are used, the martial artist automatically thinks of physical effort. However, the psychological dimension is often ignored. The brain is an organ, and as such it requires energy to function properly. Concentration, commitment, anxiety and emotional pressures of training, grading and competition increase the demands placed on the central nervous system, the brain and the spinal chord, giving a greater requirement for energy. The nervous system's demand for energy is just as great as that made by the more obvious muscular system. The coach must therefore take into account not only the physical demands of training, but psychological demands as well.

In order to understand the concept of energy use and recovery put forward in Selyle's General Adaptation to Stress Theory, it is worth looking at the 'Pie Theory' (fig.8). This shows that there is only a certain amount of energy which is available to the body. It is limited by the total amount of food consumed in a given period and the ability of the gut to assimilate the nutrients. If there is a dysfunction of the digestive system the amount of nutrients will be severely restricted. Energy does not enter the body by magic. Its availability is the direct result of a well-balanced diet. If the student has eaten a balanced diet (which is a study in itself), he will have protein, carbohydrates and fats available as materials for tissue repair, tissue increase, overfilling of energy systems or physical activity.

Carbohydrates, fats and proteins are ultimately reduced to their calorific values. With the 'Energy Pie' a given amount of energy is divided into four broad areas. Energy is required for:

- general body maintenance, repair and resistance to infection
- family and social life
- work or school
- martial arts training.

An equal distribution of available energy into the four areas gives a balanced lifestyle. However, if training makes greater demands on energy, the extra energy involved has to come from the other three areas For example, if a student is markedly overtraining, he is going to require a greater 'slice' of energy (fig.9). This might come initially from the work share. In this case the effectiveness of the student at work will be impaired, resulting in a lower standard of performance. If the student continues to increase his load, the training share of the energy pie will increase again, possibly at the expense of his social life. In such a case relationships will obviously suffer, because the student will not have the energy to maintain, develop or create new ones. Because of the amount of time spent training, the student's whole lifestyle will start to deteriorate at an ever-increasing rate. There is potential for a self-destructing mechanism to be brought into play at this stage. Because of the inbalance between work and recovery, the training will not bring about any improvement in performance. The student (who has by now lost his grip

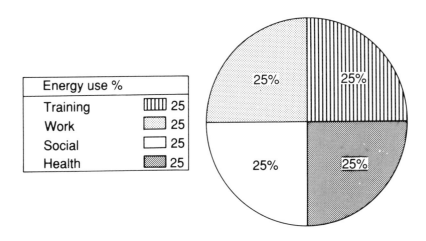

Fig. 8 Normal energy expenditure
With a well-balanced lifestyle and training programme a student should
have adequate energy for all his needs

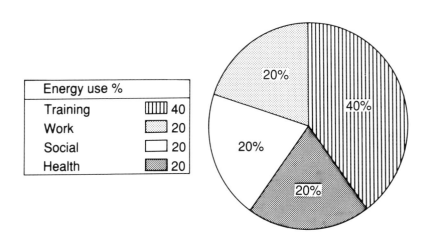

Fig. 9 Overtraining
If there is too much training, energy has to be taken from other important
areas, creating an imbalance

on reality), thinks that the only way out of this decline in performance is even more training. The problem is that the only other area which he can now take energy from is the slice responsible for his general body maintenance, tissue repair and protection against illness and disease (fig. 10). If the student takes energy from this area, the results can be both disastrous

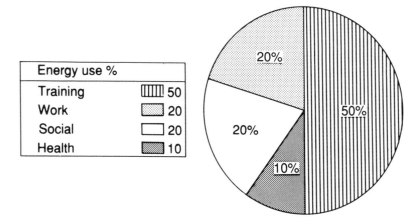

Energy use %		
Training	ⷮⷮ	50
Work	▦	20
Social	☐	20
Health	▨	10

Fig. 10 Chronic overtraining
Chronic overtraining will result in a deterioration of performance and in ill-health

and very dangerous. Continued training will bring about a rapid deterioration in performance and loss of weight, because there are no nutrients left to repair or build body tissue. Even worse, however, is the body's inability to fight off infection or disease, leaving the student totally vulnerable. Colds, influenza and general debility can rapidly lead to glandular fever and other chronic infections. If students train in this condition they may cause irreparable damage to muscles, joints, connective tissues, vital organs and body systems.

The coach must monitor students who develop an obsessive attitude towards training carefully. He must counsel his charges to maintain a sense of proportion about life in general. The coach must not encourage students to overtrain. In extreme cases medical help should be sought for the sake of the student.

5

Determining the training load

One of the most difficult tasks of the coach is assessing the training load appropriate for each student. He must take into account, among other factors:

- age
- gender
- ability
- determination
- commitment
- time available for training.

How, then, should he go about resolving this most difficult of problems?

(1) It is always better to err on the side of caution and set lower rates of work and intensities of training (fig. 11). With this approach the student will be able to cope with training and will recover in time for the

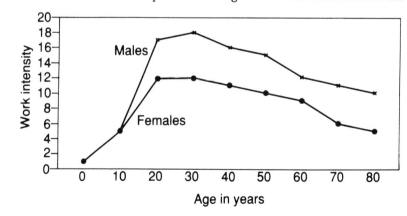

Fig. 11 Potential work rate and age
Students' potential work rates rise rapidly from their early teens to their mid-twenties. Thereafter they decline slowly. Men generally have the potential to work at higher intensities than women of the same age

next lesson. The only drawback is that the student may not improve at the optimum rate, and may become bored. Where strength is a major aspect of training, the coach must be aware of the variables (fig. 1 2). If speed is a prerequisite, the coach must once again be aware of the elements involved (fig. 1 3).

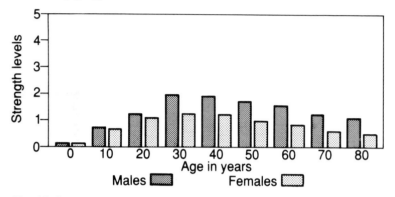

Fig. 12 Comparison of strength
Strength levels rise dramatically during the teens and mid-twenties, and decline slowly in later life. Men generally have the potential to generate more strength than women of the same age

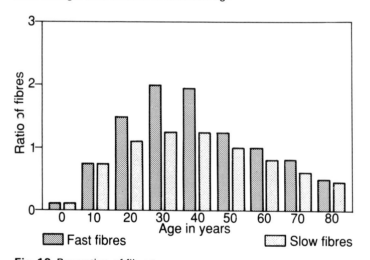

Fig. 13 Proportion of fibre types
'Fast-twitch' fibres necessary for speed of movement develop quickly from the mid-teens, to peak in the mid-twenties. Although these fast fibres decline in later years, 'slow-twitch' or endurance fibres remain in large quantities

(2) There are some signs which can give the coach feedback as to the student's ability to maintain a planned work schedule.

	IDEAL TRAINING	OVER-TRAINING	RECOVERY PERIOD
SKIN	A healthy pink	A deep red	Very pale
PERSPIRATION	Profuse in upper body	Profuse throughout the body	Profuse during sleep periods
SKILL	Deteriorates as lesson progresses	Breaks down, disorientation and confusion	Technical competence diminished
ATTITUDE	Concentration deteriorates as lesson progresses	Periods of concentration very short	Lack of ability to concentrate
HEALTH	Fatigue develops as lesson progresses	Pain in joints, muscles, head and some major organs	Sleep problems, pain and discomfort continue
COMMITMENT TO TRAINING	Enthusiastic	Need for more rest, unease felt over more intensive training	Loses interest in training

(3) It is possible that despite his years of experience, the coach may have misjudged the balance of training and recovery.

■ The amount of recovery and the associated adaptive processes can be under-estimated.

■ Training loads can be increased too quickly, not allowing for complete adaptation to the previous ones.

■ The intensity and duration of training may be beyond the ability of the student.

■ Insufficient rehabilitation may be given after injury. In the recovery process it is essential that training loads are not increased faster than the rate of healing and adaptation.

■ Particularly complicated techniques, or intensive training, require proportionally greater recovery periods.

■ Training must be balanced towards the overall improvement of the student. Over-emphasising one particular element of training will create weaknesses elsewhere.

■ Too many competitions do not allow for the maintenance or improvement of the various body systems. Put simply, excessive competition reduces the amount of training, giving an associated reduction in performance.

■ Overtraining, lack of improvement, poor training, grading and competitive results lead to a lowering of the student's confidence and his loss of faith in the coach.

■ Coach and student may be unable to keep their involvement with the martial art in perspective.

(4) Extraneous factors can have a profound effect on the effectiveness of even the best-planned training programme.

■ The student's lifestyle may not be conducive to obtaining the best possible results from training. Culprits may be:
—too little sleep
—alcohol abuse
—smoking
—abuse of illegal substances
—too much caffeine
—poor daily routine
 —too many late nights
—too much socialising
—lack of free time for recovery from training
—difficulty in maintaining body weight
—willingness to take on too many personal, social, work and training
    responsibilities, making recovery and adaptation almost impossible.

■ The domestic, social, work or school environment in which the student lives can have a major influence on his rate of progress. Among the factors to consider are the following:
—the socio-economic status of the family. This will influence living
    conditions, the provision of adequate sleeping arrangements, cloth-
    ing and meals. It will also indicate the degree of the family's likely

encouragement, its attitude and ability to support the student's involvement in the martial arts
—unhappiness in the home, at school, in studies, or at work
—additional stresses in the home, at school, in studies or at work
—the development of attitudes and behaviour inappropriate to the philosophy of the martial arts.

■ The general health of the student will influence his improvement and development. General ill-health reduces a student's ability to work and adapt to the training process.

(5) The sensitive coach can identify changes in the behaviour and general performance of a student in training, grading and competition. The student might become obviously more:
—bad-tempered
—headstrong
—unstable
—emotional
—quarrelsome
—aggressive.

Students can also be prone to rapid and violent changes in moods and behaviour. This may become noticeable when:
—self-motivation declines
—skill levels fall
—bad habits or previously corrected errors in technique recur
—general co-ordination declines
—concentration diminishes
—ability to correct training errors is reduced.

Overtraining and reduced recovery produce lower levels of performance in strength, speed, suppleness, stamina and skill. Any physical activity requires a period of recovery far longer than normal.

For the competitive student there are even more pitfalls. The desire and hunger for competition is replaced initially by unease, and then by outright fear, possibly of failure. Self-confidence rapidly diminishes and is replaced by insecurity. The will to win and persevere in the face of setbacks is reduced and often replaced by a willingness to give up. A whole series of excuses may be given for poor performance. Usually, such excuses involve everybody and everything except the student, who

The development of reaction speed and movement is an important aspect of training

is the innocent 'victim' of circumstance. Sham injury or pain can offer an easy way out for a student who finds himself in this position.

When a student has been overtraining for a sustained period of time, changes will come about in his health. These will reduce the beneficial effects of training. The student develops what is known as 'negative health'. Problems occur with:

—sleep
—patterns of eating
—vulnerability to injury and infection
—general debility and malaise.

The coach has a difficult task in ensuring that these symptoms are spotted and eradicated, by varying the training load. The coach's responsibility is to the student's welfare, above all else. Too often coaches see their students as receptors of technical knowledge and automatons, devoid of personal feelings and abilities. Coaches teach people, not techniques. The teaching of martial arts techniques is a means by which the values and philosophies of the style are passed on to the student. The techniques are not an end in themselves.

6

Developing the 'S' factors

When he is devising training programmes for his students, the coach must ask himself several important questions:
■ what are the fitness demands of the style?
■ how fit must a student be to participate in his chosen style?
■ are the fitness requirements different for various levels of ability?
■ is there a difference between the fitness required for training, grading and competition?
■ what allowances should be made in the training programme for students of different abilities, ages and sexes?

With all of these factors in mind the coach must analyse how to balance the demands of training to meet the requirements of combat style. Fitness requirements for the broad range of the martial arts will be very different. However, there will be elements of fitness common to all styles, though the emphasis will vary. In the adaptive process, or the way in which the body reacts to training, any changes are specific to the activity practised. The coach has to identify the particular aspects of fitness which he wants to develop, and must design training practices which will bring about the desired improvements. Fitness is defined by the 'S' factors:
■ speed
■ strength
■ suppleness
■ stamina
■ skill
■ (p)sychology.

Each martial art will have its own blend of these elements. For example, styles such as Thai Boxing stress hip mobility. The breaking techniques of some styles identify strength as the essential factor. Others, such as Tai Chi Chuan, place emphasis on inner energy or 'chi', in other words psychology, and do not emphasise fitness elements.

Identifying the importance of the 'S' factors

Speed

The development of speed is one of the major elements of martial arts training. It is a most complicated, and yet basic, aspect of preparation. Speed can be divided into two areas:

■ moving a single limb at speed, as in a kick, punch, block, lock, throw or takedown.

■ moving the entire body at speed, from one stance or position to another, developing a sequence of varied techniques, or changing direction of movement.

Movement at speed is a refinement of technique. Technical excellence must be mastered at moderate rates before any marked acceleration in movement patterns takes place. The tissues involved in a technique must be allowed to adapt to the stresses of a particular loading before moving on to the next. Any attempt to move a tissue, body system, limb or even the whole body at speed, before it has adapted to the loads, is a recipe for disaster. If muscles, joints, limbs or the whole body are moved at speed in the wrong pattern of movement, injury will also result.

In the martial arts speed is also used to mean reaction time. This is a very involved concept, made up from many inter-related elements.

Perception time

■ How long it takes to be aware that something is happening, or about to happen. Usually the senses of sight, sound and touch are used to detect and identify the source of activity.

Processing time

■ How long it takes to identify the nature of the movement. Is it a kick, punch, block, lock, takedown or what? The angle of attack and the speed at which it is delivered are also assessed.

Selection time

■ Having identified the nature of the attack, the appropriate defence or counter-attack has to be decided.

Movement time

■ Having selected the appropriate technique, how long does it take to perform it?

Any of these elements may take only a tiny fraction of a second, but linked together they produce an overall reaction time. The coach must devise training practices which will reduce the time it takes to process each stage. A breakdown in any one of the elements will markedly affect overall reaction time. Reacting too quickly, misinterpreting a movement, selecting an incorrect response or moving too slowly will all result in poor reaction time. Developing a concept of reaction time or any of its components can only take place over a long period.

Strength

Like speed, the concept of strength is varied and complicated. What are the similarities between the strength requirements of Tai Chi Chuan and the breaking techniques of Taekwon do? Each has its own particular emphasis. It might be useful to define the term 'strength' to make the situation a little clearer.

Strength can be defined as 'the tension or force that a muscle or group of muscles can exert against a resistance.'

This definition merely points out the rather obvious fact that when muscles contract, they produce a force. But how valuable is such an observation for the martial arts? Are muscles required to generate force in Tai Chi Chuan, as they are in Taekwon do? Will muscles work in the same way in a kata, pattern or form as in breaking techniques? Perhaps it might be helpful to redefine strength.

Maximum strength

■ The greatest tension or force which the neuro-muscular system is capable of generating in one conscious effort.

The coach has to ask himself whether his style requires that a technique is performed just *once* with *maximum* effort. If it does, as with breaking techniques, then he must design appropriate training schedules.

Relative strength

■ The greatest tension or force that the neuro–muscular system can exert as a proportion of body weight.

With this type of strength it is not the total force generated or weight lifted which is important, but how it compares with the student's own body weight. For example, Fred weighs 70 kg, (154 lbs), and can 'bench press' 140 kg (308 lb). Alf weighs 100 kg (220 lb) and can also 'bench press' 140 kg (308 lb). Both students have pressed the same weight, but Fred has managed twice his body weight, whereas Alf has not. Therefore, in proportion to their body weight, Fred is the stronger. Most martial arts require the student to move his body weight. It follows that relative strength could be an important aspect of training.

Explosive strength

■ The ability of the muscles to contract and generate force explosively.

Quality of technique should be the main object of training, followed closely by the ability to perform any technique quickly and with a variable degree of force. Within the concept of explosive strength is that of power. Power is the ability to generate the maximum force in the shortest possible time.

Speed endurance

■ The ability to continue working at maximum with an ever-increasing presence of fatigue products.

If a student is working at maximum speed, he will experience a very rapid build-up of fatigue products. Should the coach want a student to be able to work in such conditions, his training must reflect these demands.

Strength endurance

■ The ability of muscles to generate force with an ever-increasing presence of fatigue products.

As with speed endurance, it might be important to the coach that a student can maintain maximum strength and intensity for a sustained period. As training continues, the build-up of waste products increases. If this quality is what the coach desires, he must train his students accordingly.

Local muscular endurance

■ The ability of the muscles to generate force in an ever-increasing climate of fatigue at a local level.

If a student is performing many repetitions of a punching technique, by and large only his arm and shoulder muscles will become fatigued.

Mobility is an intrinsic element of technical competence in most martial arts skills

The muscles of the trunk and legs will not be worked so intensively and could continue for a great many more repetitions before they become fatigued. If the muscles of the shoulders and arms are isolated and specifically developed, the number of repetitions can be greatly increased.

The coach must identify any weak links in the form of individual muscle groups. These muscles can then be isolated and developed by specific exercises or training methods.

Suppleness

As with the other 'S' factors, the coach must have a clear understanding of suppleness, which tends to be an all-embracing notion.

Range of movement

■ The angle through which a limb or part of the body can move with respect to a specific joint, or series of joints.

The coach might want a student to have a large range of movement, for example in the hips if high kicking techniques are required. However, if joints are not isolated and worked specifically in the range required for a technique, the range of movement will not improve.

Mobility

■ The maximum range of movement that is attainable in a joint or series of joints by means of conscious, sustained effort.

Just because a joint has the potential to perform a wide range of movements does not mean it can actually do so. Injury and lack of specific training can reduce the actual movements that are possible.

Flexibility

■ The absolute range of movement that is attainable in a joint or series of joints in a momentary effort, with the help of a partner or a piece of equipment.

There is an obvious difference between a range of movement that can be sustained, as in stances, and one that can only be achieved momentarily.

Agility

■ The range of movement in a series of joints, which enables the whole body to perform complex techniques.

Many fighting techniques require that various parts of the body move in many directions, often at speed, to produce excellence. If the body is required to move as an integrated system of flexible sub-units, the training that a student receives must reflect this.

Suppleness

■ Suppleness can be used as a broad term to cover any of the previous definitions.

Suppleness will not develop without specific training. A coach should not say, 'At the moment you can only kick to mid section, so kick to mid section. In time you will be able to kick higher.' Although this might be possible, it is doubtful and wastes precious training time. The coach should ensure that specific joint-isolation exercises, possibly identifying the hips and the lower back, are included in the lesson as a matter of course, prior to kicking practices. As hip mobility increases, so will the ability to kick higher.

Stamina

Stamina is an essential aspect of all martial arts training. In fact the learning and teaching environment is based on the student's ability to work for relatively long periods of time, often quite intensively. Traditionally, martial arts lessons last between one and two hours, sometimes longer. A student will have to develop a fair degree of stamina to participate fully in the various elements of the lesson. However, during the lesson the student will not work at one sustained, low level of intensity; activities will be mainly of short duration and high intensity, with periods of rest or lighter work between them to allow the student to recover. To meet the very different demands of training, energy is provided through two systems.

The aerobic system

This ensures a constant supply of energy for a sustained period, but at a relatively low level of intensity. The student may work constantly for periods of up to an hour or longer, but if he does, the quality and intensity of his work rate will be low. Because there is a relatively low demand for energy, oxygen is made available to the active muscles and organs as fast as it is used up. When there is enough oxygen available in tissues to provide energy they are said to be working aerobically.

There is a bonus to aerobic work. When muscles produce energy in the presence of oxygen, carbon dioxide and water are produced as waste products. These have to be removed, or they will build up and hinder the efficient functioning of the muscles. The body can deal with these wastes very efficiently, and at low work levels it can remove them as fast as they are produced. The aerobic system is dependent on an efficient transport mechanism to provide oxygen and extra fuel for energy production and to remove waste products, carbon dioxide and water.

This transport system is assisted by:

■ the ability of the heart to work faster as a pump, which increases the rate of blood flow

■ the ability of blood vessels to circulate blood to active tissues efficiently, transporting nutrients and oxygen there and carbon dioxide, water and waste away

■ the ability of the lungs to work faster, assimilating oxygen from the atmosphere and directing it to circulating blood, while at the same time removing carbon dioxide

■ the ability of the blood to carry gases and nutrients.

Aerobic work is facilitated by the ability of the heart, lungs and circulating blood to function at the exact level of the work rate. The efficiency of the heart and lungs is crucial to the effectiveness of this system. Most of the major organs of the body have to adapt in similar ways, and the benefits to general health are extremely valuable.

The coach must identify methods to improve aerobic stamina if he feels that long periods of low-intensity activity are what his style requires.

The anaerobic system

Most of the activities in martial arts involve short bursts of intense physical activity. Muscles and other tissues require so much energy that oxygen cannot be transported fast enough to meet demand. However, muscles have the ability to work intensively without oxygen for short periods. The production of energy without oxygen is called anaerobic work.

There is a major drawback to anaerobic work. When muscles work without oxygen, they produce a waste product known as lactic acid. The body's transport system is not well suited to removing waste from tissues that are working at maximum. Instead of being removed as fast as it is produced, the lactic acid starts to build up, in muscles in particular, until it eventually stops them working. The build-up of lactic acid is associated with the localised stiffness and pain during and after periods of intense training.

If the coach wants his students to train intensively, the anaerobic system has to be developed. It is very different from aerobic energy production. The coach must look carefully at the intensity of the training load for students with different levels of conditioning (fig. 14).

The problem is confused slightly more by the fact that both systems work in a co-ordinated fashion. The aerobic system is characterised by an efficient transport system, and this is vital to solving the problem of anaerobic work, lactic acid. Anaerobic work is eventually reduced by the build-up of waste products. Once the student has stopped being active, his body's transport system can restore the situation. It does this in two ways:

■ it speeds up the removal of waste products—in particular lactic acid
■ it brings large amounts of oxygen to the tissues, which help break down any remaining lactic acid into more disposable products. (The amount of oxygen required to return muscle and other tissue to maximum efficiency is often referred to as the 'oxygen debt'.)

The efficiency of the transport system will affect the rate of recovery from intense work and allow a student to repeat the activity again if necessary. Before intensive training can commence the aerobic work capacity of a student must be improved. This will increase his ability to remove waste products and speed up his recovery after intensive work.

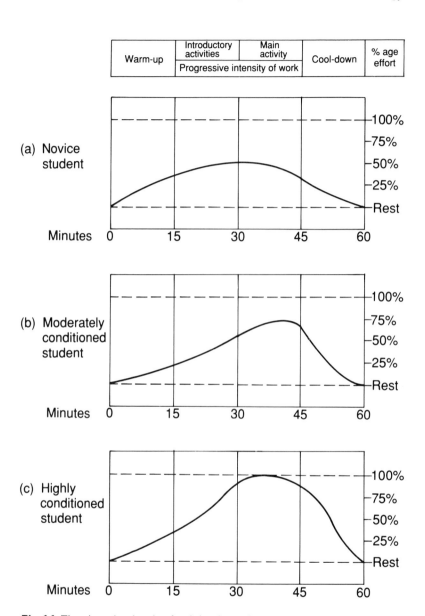

Fig.14 The changing levels of training intensity
(a) Novice students should not be stressed at levels above 50 per cent
(b) As students become better-conditioned, they are able to cope with more intensive training of up to 75 per cent
(c) Highly conditioned students are able to work at levels of up to 100 per cent for short periods

In the training, grading and competition of martial arts there are clearly identified energy demands, which require interaction between the aerobic and the anaerobic systems.

The anaerobic systems

Energy demands are of the following type.
(1) Instantaneous—less than a second—as with a breaking technique, or one effort at maximum.
(2) Very short-term—up to 5 seconds—as with a short sequence of techniques performed with maximum effort.
(3) Medium-term—up to 15 seconds—as with a sustained sequence of techniques performed with maximum effort.
(4) Long-term—up to 60 seconds—as with sustained and constant activity at maximum effort

The co-ordinated anaerobic and aerobic systems

Energy demands are of the following type.
(1) Short-term—up to three minutes—intense sustained activity; sparring or competitive bout.
(2) Medium-term—up to five minutes—intense, continuous and sustained activity; grading; squad training.

The aerobic system

Energy demands are of the following type
(1) Long duration, low intensity of work—lasts as long as is required; very important in the recovery process.
The coach's difficult task is to identify the energy demands of his fighting style and create a training programme which will develop them. The adaptive process is highly specific. Developing the aerobic system will not improve immediate energy availability, although it will increase the rate of recovery. Training and adaptation must be specific to the needs of the style and the student.

Skill

The development of martial arts skills and an understanding of the philosophy of a fighting style is the result of many years of practice and progressive training. It is widely accepted that an individual reaches the peak of his physical potential at around the age of 25. However, this may not apply to martial artists. All fighting styles require a degree of speed, strength, suppleness and stamina, although the particular 'mix' involved will be highly specific to each style. Unlike other sporting or leisure activities, the martial arts require an understanding of the application and philosophy of a technique. This may be far more important than the age and physical capabilities of a student in the production of technical excellence and effectiveness (fig. 15).

Martial arts skills are learnt in the following stages.

Stage 1—basic pattern of the movement

Stage 2—crude but recognisable attempts of a technique

Stage 3—technical refinement

Stage 4—technical adaptation

Stage 5—physiological adaptation.

This skill-development process means that in lessons there is a need for:

■ repetition of movements. This will enable them to be learned or perfected

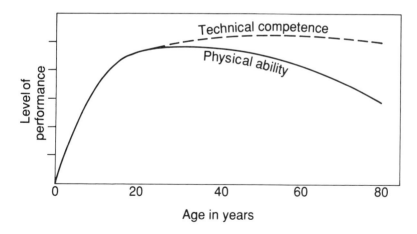

Fig. 15 Age and martial arts competence
The mix of speed, strength, stamina and suppleness is unique to each style and technique. However, as technical competence increases, the contribution of the 'physical' to overall performance becomes less

In all training the emphasis must be placed on the development of technical excellence, rather than on strength, speed, power or mobility

■ development of easy and fluid body movements. This requires time and is dependent on the ability and the commitment of the student

■ emphasis on the development of correct patterns of movement, rather than speed, strength or force.

The coach must judge how much time he is going to apportion to the learning and refinement of new skills, and the application of established ones. This aspect of coaching the martial arts—the acquisition, refinement and application of techniques—is simultaneously the most important and the most difficult to organise in a training programme (fig. 16).

One other interesting aspect of the learning process is the active involvement of the coach. Because of the various levels of ability among his students, the coach has to move about the class. The way in which he makes effective use of his time will have an influence on his students' rate of learning (fig. 17).

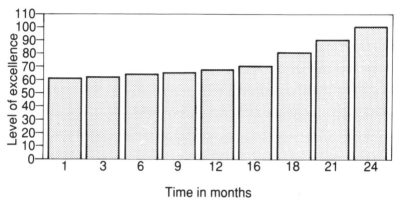

Fig. 16 The rate of learning
Students will quickly achieve a working grasp of a technique. However, only supervised practise over a lengthy period will improve quality of movement

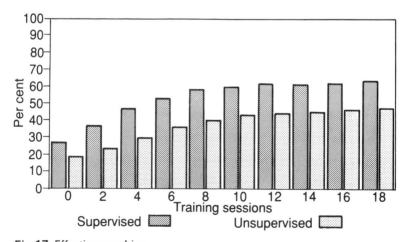

Fig. 17 Effective coaching
To ensure effective learning, the coach has to give each student adequate supervision

Psychology

A story is often told in sports science circles of the young American woman who was driving her son to school when one of the tyres on the car burst. While she was changing the wheel, the jack failed, pinning her son, who was lending a hand, underneath the car. In panic she took hold of the bumper and actually managed to lift the car up, allowing the child to crawl out. It was later calculated that the woman had lifted a load of over a ton (1.02 metric tonnes), causing herself serious injury in the process.

In a moment of desperation, panic and desire to protect her son, the American woman was oblivious to normal physical 'safety mechanisms' such as discomfort or pain, and focused all her energy into one massive effort. There are many examples of similar feats of strength in the martial arts, though thankfully they are not triggered by such circumstances.

Concentration, visualisation, meditation, mental rehearsal, focus or the utilisation of 'chi' are controlled forms that use this massive reserve of inner energy which we possess. Physical safety mechanisms are also there, to prevent injury and damage to the body. However, it is still possible to tap these reserves in a safe way. All training involves both mind and body, and part of the training process is to push back psychological barriers. If a student has experienced a certain level of training—be it mental or physical—he knows he can push himself a little further in the next session, and he does. If a student has confidence in his style, coach, training and technique, he will progress towards the extremes of his potential. The role of the coach in creating this personal belief, self-confidence, attitude, state of mind—call it what you will—is vital and self-evident. All training should be directed towards creating the right physical and mental conditions for personal development.

7

Planning training

It is all well and good to discuss the theoretical elements of training programmes. However, it is the coach who will have to put theory into practice. He must firstly identify the philosophy, intellectual and physical demands of his style and all the variables which are applicable to each student (fig.18). Secondly, he must identify the long-, medium- and short-term targets that he wants his programme to achieve.

Long-term planning

The coach may see the involvement of a student as a very long process, possibly even lasting a lifetime. More realistically, though, he will see a year as a long-term unit. Before any constructive planning can begin, all the major events in the year need to be set out. These will include gradings; national, regional and association competitions; squad training; training camps, and courses.

Once these key dates are set out, the coach can plan his work so that his students will be in the best possible state of preparation for an event. The use of a year planner (fig.19) can be invaluable.

Intermediate targets

These can be regarded as building-blocks which make up the year, especially for lower-grade students. Normally students in the elementary stages of development grade every 12 weeks. The year can be seen as four blocks of 12 weeks. The remaining four weeks are taken up with other activities.

The idea of a 12-week period between grading follows modern ideas about the effects of training. It also follows current practice in the medical world. For example, fractured limbs are expected to be load-bearing after

	Speed	Reaction time	Mobility	Flexibility	Agility	Maximum strength	Relative strength	Explosive strength	Aerobic endurance	Anaerobic endurance	Speed endurance	Strength endurance	Local muscular endurance	Skill
Aikido														10
Hapkido														10
Iaido														10
Judo														10
Jujitsu														10
Karate														10
Kendo														10
Kung fu														10
Ninjutsu														10
Shorinji kempo														10
Sumo														10
Tae kwando														10
Tai chi chuan														10
Tang soo do														10
Thai boxing														10
Full contact														10
Training variables														
Training														
Grading														
Competition														
Age														
Gender														
Ability														

six weeks, and able to withstand light training after 12 weeks. Where giving blood is concerned, some authorities require a minimum of six weeks between donations, while others require 12. These periods of six and 12 weeks are very important. In the body's adaptation to training it takes six weeks for measurable physiological changes to occur, and a further six weeks for them to be established.

Although the 12-week grading period is an acceptable timescale, there is a problem. The minimum period of preparation is six weeks. Two hard sessions before an important event will have no physiological benefits, although there might be psychological ones. In his planning the coach must therefore consider dates and plan back six or 12 weeks or longer, as the case may be.

There are clear stages in the body's adaptation to training. They are as follows.

Stage 1—development of endurance
Stage 2—development of general strength
Stage 3—development of specific strength
Stage 4—development of mobility
Stage 5—development of speed
Stage 6—development of skill.

These stages of development do not mean that in the early part of the 12-week period students only practise endurance activities. Throughout the 12-week programme, in every lesson, students will be involved in the development of all of the elements of performance identified. Each stage will emphasise one particular component of fitness. The shift in the balance of training follows the pattern described below.

Stage 1—novice students need to develop basic aerobic and anaerobic fitness to allow them to train for the whole lesson. Students who have been graded previously will also need to increase their level of aerobic

Left
Fig. 18 Planning training
The various elements of training are identified at the top of the diagram. As an exercise the coach should first find his activity down the left-hand side, and secondly, on a scale of 1 to 10, place a number under the appropriate element of training, to identify its importance for that style. Coaches should assume that skill would score 10 for all styles. The exercise can be repeated to suit the requirements of training, grading, competition, age and gender. Ability to understand the differing needs of students is required on the part of the coach

Month – Week commencing																							
Week training year	1	2	3	4	5	6	7	8	9	10	11	12	13	14	15	16	17	18	19	20	21	22	23

Planned competition/Grading programme

Date	Venue	Competition/Grading

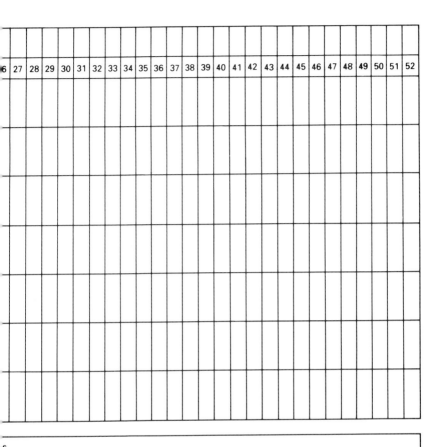

6	27	28	29	30	31	32	33	34	35	36	37	38	39	40	41	42	43	44	45	46	47	48	49	50	51	52

s

Fig. 19 Planning the year
The coach should identify major competitions, gradings, and national and local events, so that he can plan training around them

and anaerobic fitness, to meet the increased demands of the next grade. It takes time for tissues to adapt to, and tolerate, increased work loads.

Stage 2—now he is able to train for the lesson, the student must increase his general level of strength to allow his muscles, joints, tendons, ligaments and other tissues to cope with increased loadings. If muscles in particular are subjected to intense loads without preparation, the risk of injury will be greatly increased.

Stage 3—with the general increase in the body's strength, specific parts, particularly muscles, joints, tendons and ligaments, must be isolated to tolerate higher work loads and prepared for the extreme forces with which they will have to cope in training, grading or competition. General strengthening must be the basis of preparation for more intensive strength development. If ill-prepared tissues are subject to extreme loads, injury is almost inevitable.

Stage 4—most techniques require a specific range of movement in a joint or series of joints. There must always be a period of general mobility, often associated with strengthening work, preceding specific joint-isolation activities. Tissues have to be stretched gently and accustomed to tension before they can be exposed to extreme movements.

Stage 5—any movement that requires speed needs muscles which contract quickly to produce the required motion in a joint. Specific strengthening has to precede any attempt to improve speed. Rapid movements will place extreme loads on joints, muscles and other connective tissues, so initially both general and highly specific strengthening must take place.

Stage 6—though techniques are learned and developed from the first lesson of the 12-week period, they are refined by crude, trial and error efforts to technical excellence. When they are performed at the highest possible standard, all techniques require that the student possesses specific endurance, strength, suppleness and speed. As individual components improve, so will technical competence. A technique can only be practised to an extreme degree of skill once all the elements that contribute to it have been achieved.

The coach should be aware of levels of skill acquisition.

Level 1—**have a go!**

In the early stages of learning there is much trial and error.

The coach must be aware of the stages in the development of skilful movement patterns

Level 2—**crude reproduction**
> A basic, but identifiable pattern of movement occurs.

Level 3—**refinement of technique**
> Errors are corrected and the movement becomes more refined.

Level 4—**establishment of standard of performance**
> The movement pattern becomes 'grooved in'.

Level 5—**physical adaptation**
> Continued practice brings about specific adaptation of body systems.

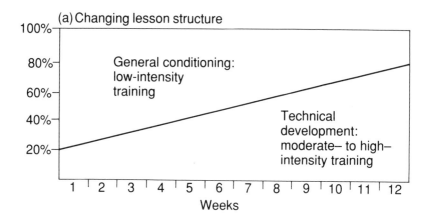

(a) Changing lesson structure

General conditioning: low-intensity training

Technical development: moderate– to high-intensity training

Weeks

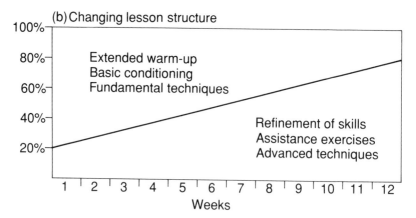

(b) Changing lesson structure

Extended warm-up
Basic conditioning
Fundamental techniques

Refinement of skills
Assistance exercises
Advanced techniques

Weeks

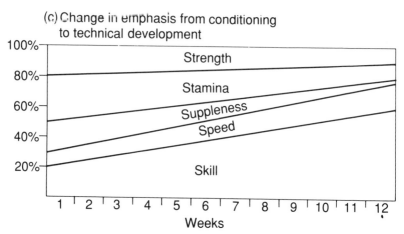

(c) Change in emphasis from conditioning to technical development

Strength

Stamina

Suppleness

Speed

Skill

Weeks

Obviously the body will adapt to produce a technique only if it is worked in exactly the way required. Thereafter, repetition of the technique will bring about the specific adaptation of the various limbs involved.

The coach has to be aware of a change in emphasis during the 12-week training period and plan accordingly. The difficulty lies in balancing the programme. How does one develop aerobic and anaerobic endurance, for example? Repetitions of techniques will develop endurance, both during activity and in the recovery phase afterwards. More specific activities, such as running, may also be introduced. The balance of work, intensity and recovery must be manipulated throughout the period. There does not have to be a change in traditional lessons, but a gradual shift in emphasis is necessary to meet the requirements of particular phases (fig.20).

The important thing to consider is the change in emphasis from general preparation, where there is quantity of activity at a low level of intensity. As the weeks progress, there will be more intense, quality training, but with a decreased quantity of work (fig.21). In practice this might work as follows.

Early lessons:	Final lessons:
—extended warm-up	—revision of techniques
—introductory activities	—new techniques
—conditioning exercises	—specific drills
—conditioning games.	—specific exercises
	—class work
	—group work
	—partner work
	—repetition.

Left
Fig. 20 The change of emphasis in training in a 12-week period prior to grading
(a) There should be a general change in the emphasis of training, from general conditioning to technical excellence
(b) Initially, basic techniques should be taught, especially with novices. As techniques become refined, more advanced skills can be introduced
(c) Though it is often difficult to identify the proportions of 'S' factors involved in training, a practical change in emphasis should take place

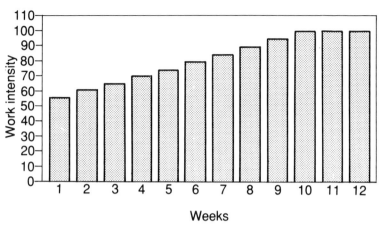

Fig. 21 The training period
As training progresses from weeks one to 12, the intensity of work should increase

In order to see how this change in emphasis occurs, it is useful to look at the final link in planning.

Short-term targets

The smallest, and perhaps the most important part of the whole planning process, is the structure and content of individual lessons. As we have already seen, there is a clear shift in the content of lessons from the beginning of the 12-week period to the end. For most novices an hour is long enough for a lesson. One-and-a-half hours will require great powers of endurance, which they will not yet have. Lessons of one-and-a-half hours or longer should be given only to advanced, well-conditioned and committed students.

Early lessons might have the following structure (the approximate time given for each section is based on a 60-minute lesson):
■ warm up—longer than normal, thorough and extensive (15 minutes)
■ introductory activities—exercises as precursors to specific techniques, for example hip mobility exercises if kicks are being practised (5 minutes)

■ skill work—one or two techniques are taught and practised on a 'have-a-go' basis (15 minutes)
■ conditioning work—general and specific conditioning exercises, as required (10 minutes)
■ games or 'fun' training—(10 minutes)
■ cool down—(5 minutes).

As the skill phase continues, the coach will review the previous lessons and introduce new techniques. This section should gradually become larger as the lessons progress. As more time is devoted to skills, less time can be spent on other areas. This may not be the problem it might seem, since it is through the repetition of skills that endurance, strength, suppleness, speed and application will develop in the way required.

Later lessons might have the following structure:

■ warm-up—progressive exercise of the larger muscle groups (5 minutes)
■ introductory activities—continuing the warm-up to include specific muscles and joints (5 minutes)
■ skill work—beginning with low-intensity, basic techniques, which increase progressively and systematically (35 minutes)
■ conditioning work—as required (5 minutes)
■ games or 'fun' training—(5 minutes)
■ cool down—(5 minutes).

8

Training theory – the ten commandments

When devising training programmes appropriate to his chosen style and philosophy, the coach must bear in mind several factors.

Versatility

The essence of a training programme is variety. A coach should include a wide range of activities, not only to achieve the purpose of the schedule, but to add interest and 'fun' to training. With the correct balance of work, recovery and enjoyment a student will not only achieve the desired results but experience the pleasures of training and the company of others. This will also help him to develop a sense of perspective about life in general. The old adage, 'All work and no play makes Jack a dull boy', is especially true of a biased and repetitive programme.

A student should be exposed to the various aspects of his chosen style. He will not master them all, but they will improve his attitude, commitment and participation. The astute coach will also acknowledge that activities outside the martial arts have much to offer. For example, jogging provides endurance, weight-training develops strength and gymnastics improve agility generally, while soccer, rugby, netball and hockey all encourage team spirit. Variety in his other activities will give the student a sense of proportion. He will develop his all-round talents and abilities, which will be supportive and reinforce the specific element of the martial arts which he and the coach have selected.

However, there will come a time when a student needs to devote more training to the specific. The coach must devise a programme which allows periods of fun and non-specific activity to lighten the training load and add an extra dimension of enjoyment. This will increase the student's desire to endure the greater efforts and commitment created by specialisation.

Health promotion

Any training programme must take into account the age, gender and ability of the students. The most important things a programme can achieve are first and foremost personal skills, which will allow the individual to make a valuable contribution to society in general. Next come the development of general health and well-being and the development of fighting skills.

There are quite clear stages in training when loads increase. However, some students may be quite happy to remain at the particular level which suits their commitment and aspirations. The levels of training load are:

■ active relaxation—training has a light-hearted and social dimension
■ a slight increase in the intensity of work
■ a medium intensity of work, which makes demands on the cardio-vascular and neuro-muscular systems
■ a sub-maximum intensity of work, which makes strong loading on the major body systems, with fatigue after training
■ peak loadings, which require a high intensity of work with fatigue produced during each period of effort.

In planning the lesson the coach has to identify which level of intensity is appropriate to each student. This is not the easiest of tasks.

Effectiveness

Better results can be achieved in training, grading or competition through improved condition, co-ordination and technical competence. The overall level of technical ability can be improved if the coach ensures that the following are included in his lessons:

■ general conditioning
■ assistance exercises
■ skill drills.

Martial arts lessons should not be solely concerned with combat skills, though of course they are of vital importance. There has to be a balance in activities to provide technical development as well as specific improvements in speed, strength, suppleness and psychology. These will enhance the student's overall performance and general fitness.

For all students, particularly youngsters, the martial arts help to develop many personal, interpersonal and social skills

Personality

For improvement in their selected styles, students should be aware of the need for:
- discipline
- collaboration
- co-operation
- self-reliance
- independent activity.

Individuals operate in the wider concept of society, and this should be reflected in training. If a student is to get the best out of his lessons, he must develop his social skills, which will also be prized by society in general. This aspect of training is very often ignored by the coach. He must remember that the student has a responsibility to his total development as a person, not just to his fighting skills or fitness.

Repetition

By gradually increasing the number of repetitions, movement patterns and skills become automatic. However, strength, speed, stamina and suppleness are only improved by a limited number of repetitions, and these have to be carefully balanced with recovery. The actual number of repetitions cannot be increased arbitrarily, since extreme loadings will bring about fatigue. This will, in turn, affect the quality of movement. Rest or recovery is a vital part of the training process. Neglecting rest will result in overtraining. The prudent balance of work and recovery is the hallmark of a successful coach.

Repetition by itself will not necessarily bring about improvements in technical excellence. A student might be repeating a movement incorrectly, thereby 'grooving-in' a bad technique. Repetition of movement patterns is only beneficial if the coach gives his student regular feedback about good points and errors that need to be corrected. In a large class the coach must be constantly vigilant.

Repetition of any technique is only of benefit if the coach gives positive feedback and identifies the errors to be corrected

'S' factors

In any training programme there must be a correct balance of strength, speed, suppleness, stamina, skill and psychology. The exact balance of these factors is unique to a particular style and the commitment and ability of each student.

The coach has to identify the balance of the 'S' factors for his chosen combat style. This balance will vary with training, grading and competition.

Durability

Any work programme in the martial arts requires a training structure. This will ensure that established skills, co-ordination and general condition are retained over a long period without any deterioration in quality.

Students cannot practise every technique during each lesson. The coach's programme must promote the development of individual techniques as they become important, while at the same time ensuring that others do not deteriorate.

Progression

Progression is linked closely to the principle of repetition, and all technical training must prescribe to the following:

- techniques must develop from simple to complex movements
- techniques must develop from easy to difficult movements
- techniques must progress from the known to the unknown.

The coach must carefully structure his training programme so that techniques are learned sequentially. Acquiring basic technique is the starting-point for a more complex one. Students need to feel confident about what they are doing or are asked to do. Being able to perform a single movement gives them confidence to attempt a more complicated one. It also gives insight into what the technique and the coaching require of them.

Age

The coach must be aware of, and make allowances for, the fact that age affects not only performance but also the training process. All work schedules in the martial arts must cater for the different abilities of various age groups.

Gender

The coach must be aware of the way in which students of both sexes respond to the training load. Men and women differ in their adaptation to training. The coach must modify work schedules accordingly.

9

Planning the programme

It is vital that the coach builds various phases or emphases into his training programme (fig.22). These should fall into four main areas:
■ the preparation phase, sometimes erroneously called the 'off season'
■ the transition or pre-season phase
■ the competition or season phase
■ the active recovery period.

The preparation phase

Many coaches see this as a non-active period, when there is little in the way of intensive training. Although the competition phase may seem a long way away, much useful work can still take place during this time. The main theme should be general conditioning, preparing the student for the more intensive work loads to come. Training should be varied, with emphasis on aerobic endurance, general strength, local muscular endurance and general mobility. This period also offers coach and student the opportunity to identify any weaknesses or major problems in technique and performance which appeared during the previous competition phase. There is plenty of time to correct errors or to work on specific aspects of fitness or technique at this stage, without the pressure of competition.

This phase in the training cycle is in many ways a foundation for the work that follows. Although it may seem low-key and not too demanding in terms of quality or quantity of effort, it is nevertheless vital to the success of the competition period. Because this phase seems so undemanding, many coaches believe that the total volume of work can be crammed into a very short but intensive period just prior to competition. This notion is not only wrong; it overlooks the purpose of the preparation phase, in which the student's body adapts to new and higher

The coach must make subtle changes to the training load during any programme of work if students are to achieve their potential in grading or competition

Right
Fig. 22 Planning the programme
An annual training programme can be broken down into four components: preparation, transition, competition and active recovery. As training progresses, the student's level of performance should improve systematically and progressively. This diagram shows how important it is for training to be planned so that the peak period of performance coincides with major competitions, gradings or events

Preparation				Transition			Competition			Active recovery	
Oct	Nov	Dec	Jan	Feb	Mar	Apr	May	Jun	Jul	Aug	Sep

Conditioning: development of
– endurance
– strength
– flexibility
– co-ordination

Development of skills
– basic skills
– advanced skills
– sparring
– kata

Competiton
– individual
– team

'Gentle' training

Development of competition – specific preparation, tactics and strategies

Improving level of performance

recovery

Basic standard of performance

Competitions

club
inter-club
city
county
regional
national
international

physical demands. Any adaptation takes time, and intensive activity which stresses poorly adapted or unadapted tissues is potentially injurious.

During this part of the training year the coach and student have an opportunity to explore other facets of preparation, which might not be immediately obvious. One of the key elements in the overall preparation of a martial artist is the development of physical fitness and technical competence. However, the psychological dimension is often forgotten. If the student cannot adapt successfully to the stresses of training, grading or competition besides a multitude of other personal, social, emotional, financial, occupational or academic ones as well, he will not succeed, no matter what his level of physical and technical competence. The preparation phase offers a student the opportunity to develop mental skills— such as concentration, relaxation and visualisation—as part of his training in technical excellence.

The transition phase

With most sporting activities the pre-competition phase begins approximately eight weeks before the main competition period. It is a time when the general, physical conditioning of the preparation phase is developed more specifically and geared towards the requirements and demands of training, grading and competition.

Strength training slowly changes its emphasis from general conditioning to more specific exercises, involving particular muscle groups. The transition phase enables weaknesses to be eliminated and muscle groups and specific parts of the body to be conditioned so that they can withstand the intensive loadings of performance.

There is a similar change in the emphasis on endurance. During the preparation phase the main aim is to raise the student's general level of fitness to withstand the demands of training, which are mainly aerobic. During the pre-competition phase training moves from low-intensity, long-duration activities to shorter, more intensive work. The development of anaerobic endurance, which is what this kind of work involves, is again preparation for the demands of performance. Various strategies can be employed by the coach to develop the specific endurance required, such as mixing different intensities of work with rest periods.

During this phase the balance of training should shift to allow more time for the development and refinement of skills. It would be unwise to regard physical conditioning as the main purpose of training at this stage. As the student progresses towards the competition phase, the balance of training must shift to mastering techniques. When the student is refining these techniques it is a good time for him to apply mental skills developed in the preparation phase. This will ensure that he is in the best frame of mind to execute movements in any situation.

The early competitive phase

This phase is a logical extension and refinement of the pre-competitive phase. Training is geared totally towards the stresses of combat, and all activity is 'activity specific'. The development of strength, speed, power, flexibility and endurance is aimed specifically at the requirements of the activity. The emphasis in training load shifts even further towards the refinement of personal skills and, where appropriate, tactics. Training is modified in intensity and general structure so that it resembles the physical and mental stresses of a competitive environment. Mental skills learned and developed in the early phases should be maintained. Even if the time available is limited, they must be included.

All training loads are high, placing intense stress on all the body systems. With such demanding activity the number of training units per week should be reduced to allow adequate recovery. Such sessions are anaerobic in nature, and the coach should vary training strategies to create effective programmes.

The competitive phase

This phase may be designed to last for one sustained, or two short periods, allowing a rest in between. Which ever option the coach selects in his programme will depend on the nature of the competitive season or grading requirements. Training is now *totally* geared towards the very specific demands of the competitive environment. Within each training unit it should be possible to work on the weaknesses in technique or strategy which appeared in the previous competition or simulated competition. Training loads should be of the highest possible intensity, with emphasis on speed and power. Work must be geared totally towards high quality, low intensity activities but the need to maintain a basic level of fitness must also be catered for. There is also a need to maintain mental skills.

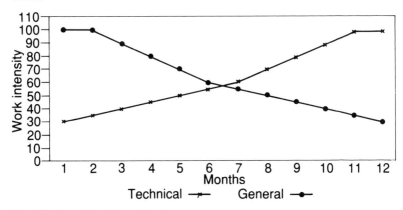

Fig. 23 Annual training plan 1
As training progresses throughout the year there is a shift in emphasis, from general to technical training

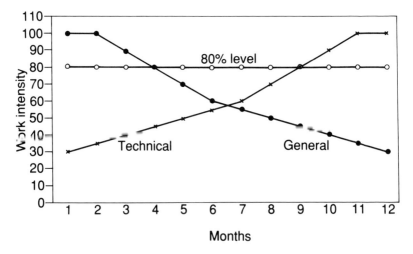

Fig. 24 Annual training plan 2
It should be possible for a student to maintain an overall standard of performance of approximately 80 per cent throughout the year. However, the extra 20 per cent required for major events can only be achieved and maintained for short periods, approximately six weeks in 12 months. It is vital that training for peaks of general or technical conditioning is planned to coincide with the appropriate events

The recovery phase

Just as important as the competitive phase is the recovery phase. This valuable period in the training programme allows the various body systems to recover from the rigours of intensive work. It is not a period of rest or inactivity, but one of active recuperation. Students should be encouraged to participate in other activities within the style and other sports or leisure pursuits. It is important that the level of conditioning should not fall too low, while at the same time the student's enthusiasm to train in the next year's programme should be kindled.

Fig.23 shows a systematic and progressive shift in training emphasis throughout the year. This is seen more clearly in fig.24.

I O
—

Long-term planning

A lesson is only of value if its contents are part of a long-term programme. Lessons which are out of sequence or 'off-the-cuff' are not only of little value but also indicate a lack of forethought, planning and commitment on the part of the coach. With most martial arts fixed periods and dates have to be considered when looking at the long term. Most styles have a set period between gradings. This may vary between three and 12 months, or longer. By setting down a programme of work the conscientious coach can decide which techniques should be taught, when and how they should follow each other sequentially. A plan formulated by the coach for each grade within a class will ensure that all students derive the maximum benefit from a lesson.

The long-term plan

The coach has to study the syllabus appropriate to each grade within a class carefully. Some governing bodies do not have even a 'minimum' syllabus. Once techniques have been identified, the coach must include them in the appropriate week's lesson. When he has repeated this procedure for all grades he will know exactly which techniques need to be taught in each lesson. This can be of great help in devising an individual lesson plan.

Having identified all the techniques which have to be taught in each lesson, the coach is able to consider how he will teach them. For example, if there are five different grades in a class and all of them have to learn and develop a particular kick, punch, throw, block or lock, these techniques can be taught to the whole class. There may be techniques which are common to two grades, and others which are relevant only to the other grades. The coach must then teach two groups, each working on a common skill. If different techniques are required by each grade, the class can be split up into grade groups, each working on the techniques appropriate to them.

This practice is suitable for the teaching of new skills, and it can also be used to review and refine those already learned. The entire programme should identify what the work is, and how each lesson fits into the whole. From this the coach can quite easily construct a lesson plan.

The structure of a lesson should be dynamic. Consider a novice student, working on a 12-week programme to grade to a higher level. His early lessons should emphasise warm-up and introductory activities. The student may not be prepared for the demands of the techniques which he will need to learn and perfect to achieve the appropriate grading. Particular exercises may have to be included to develop the specific 'S' factors that he requires for technical excellence. Novice students in particular have to be eased gently into martial arts training. Initially there may be emphasis on games and 'fun' activities to create the desire to train and learn.

II

Planning training

When devising a teaching programme the coach must clearly identify what he expects his students to learn. This ultimate purpose is described as the 'aim' of training. The aim represents the 'ideal' purpose, a goal which we may strive towards, but will never reach. In the struggle to achieve the 'ideal' the coach has to identify attainable targets. These can be useful indicators of progression, or the level of a student's achievement.

With any systematic and progressive long-term training regime there must be an underlying target, or series of targets, to achieve. The coach has to decide which targets are most important. For instance, is the training solely designed to bring about an increase in the number and quality of martial arts skills? Or is the underlying philosophy of the martial art to prepare a student for life, help him become a valuable member of society and develop in him an appreciation of the cultural, moral, emotional, and spiritual heritage of his martial art and of mankind in general?

The mnemonic MARTIAL ART can be useful for the coach to remember when he is identifying some of the more important goals

The coach has to:

M   Measure
Measure any improvements in the quality of technical or personal standards.

A   Action
Identify a specific target and a plan of action to achieve it.

R   Realistic
Set realistic targets which the student can attain.

T   Training
Devise a plan of action before training starts.

I   Intermediate
Identify intermediate training in the form of attainable targets.

A   Acceptance
Encourage students to accept the demands of the learning process.
L   Learn
Motivate students to learn and improve.

A   Application
Encourage students to apply themselves to the work programme.
R   Responsibility
Explain to students that they must accept responsibility for their technical and personal standards.
T   Time
Be aware that the amount of time spent training is proportional to improvement goals.

If all the objectives of the training programme are MARTIAL ART ones, there will be a greater chance of success for both students and coach. Obviously some elements are easily measured, for example the number of press-ups a student does. However, the qualitative assessment of technical excellence does present difficulties.

When devising a plan for a group or an individual, it is important that the purpose of training is identified. The coach has to recognise the requirements of a particular martial art, and the abilities and limitations which a student possesses. There has to be a great deal of care and honesty involved in the setting of targets. If they are too high, the student will be constantly frustrated; if too low, he will be bored. The coach has to assess how the student and the art can interrelate in the most mutually advantageous way.

The coach must devise a programme which has an ideal, long-term aim, but which can also be broken down into intermediate targets. These targets consist of a number of elements. In practice the overall programme might work out as follows.

The long-term aim of the training programme

- The appreciation of the philosophy of the martial art.
- The development of the student socially and intellectually.
- The acquisition and development of technical excellence and its application.

With a well-constructed training programme a student can achieve the high level of control, skill and personal development associated with the martial arts

The intermediate targets

- The aquisition of grades in a systematic and progressive manner.
- Exposure to the various aspects of training, grading and competition.

Short-term targets

- The individual lessons, competitions or training opportunities to which students are exposed.

In planning lessons the coach has to set out long-term targets, intermediate targets and short-term targets. Using MARTIAL ART he will be able to monitor students in their attainment of the 'ideal', and will be able to modify the programme if any adjustments are necessary.

12

Fitness tests and measurements

In the construction of any training schedule the coach must consider several important factors—the age, gender, weight and height of a student, and also his attitude and commitment to a particular fighting style. Although all martial arts philosophies aim at the overall development of the student as a valuable member of society, the training process is the means by which this is achieved. The outward manifestation of this process is the quality of technical excellence. This in its turn is influenced by the 'S' factors. Although the coach and the governing body of a particular style can regularly assess a student through the grading process, this can only take place infrequently. In the lower grades of most martial arts assessments can be made every three months. However, as the students attain higher standards the period between gradings increases from three to six and then to 12 months, or longer. How, then, can a coach ensure that his students are progressively and systematically improving? A regular programme of appraisal is essential. This might be informal, for instance if the coach monitors the student during a lesson, or by more formal assessment. Such appraisals should take place at least once a month, and ideally involve both technical and physical progress. The time given to the evaluation of students should be built into the training programme.

Tests and measurements can also be an invaluable source of information, for the following reasons.

(1) They give the coach a clear understanding of the fitness level of new students. From such information he can construct programmes to meet their needs.

(2) They highlight particular weaknesses or strengths in any of the 'S' factors.

(3) They identify the progress (or lack of it) that a student has made since the last testing session.

(4) They confirm the effectiveness of a training programme, or give the coach an indication where changes should be made.

(5) Students need to have feedback. Tests can be a positive incentive, since students are measured against themselves.

(6) The results of regular testing and measuring can be of immense value to the coach. They help to identify negative trends in individual students. These might be due to overtraining, or to physical or psychological problems.

(7) When progress can be observed, students develop a more positive approach to training, to the style in general and to their coach in particular.

To help the coach with his programme this book includes a 'fitness decathlon'. It is designed to assess major aspects of all the 'S' factors which are relevant to the martial arts. It is not possible to identify which scores are appropriate to specific martial arts, since the demands of individual styles vary so much. The coach must use his knowledge and understanding of a style to identify which particular aspect of fitness is needed.

Like the decathlon event in track and field athletics, ten tests are included in the 'fitness decathlon'. They cover aspects of strength, speed, endurance and flexibility.

The Vertical Jump

The right-handed student stands with the right side of his body close to the wall. He extends his right arm up above his head as high as possible, and makes a mark with his fingertips (fig.25). Wet or chalk-covered fingers are ideal. The student then jumps as high as possible, stretching the right arm high up the wall and making another mark with the fingertips (figs.26 and 27). The distance between the two marks is then measured (fig.28). The student has three attempts and the best effort is recorded. This test measures the student's leg strength, as well as how high he can jump. It also indicates the degree of power that the student can generate in one maximum effort.

If the student is left-handed, he should perform the test with his left side to the wall. However, the coach can also ask a student to perform the test with first his right side to the wall, and then his left. This indicates the

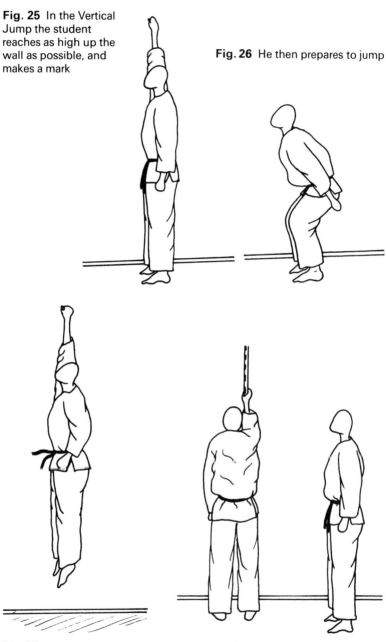

Fig. 25 In the Vertical Jump the student reaches as high up the wall as possible, and makes a mark

Fig. 26 He then prepares to jump

Fig. 27 At the high point of his jump he makes a mark

Fig. 28 The distance between the two marks is measured

degree of possible imbalance between the two sides, which may be important.

The Four-Times-10-Metre (Yard) Shuttle Run

Two lines are drawn on the floor 10 metres apart. In most training areas badminton, volleyball or basketball court markings will usually provide suitable lines and distances. The student stands with his feet behind the 'start' line, with one foot forward just behind the line (fig.29). When he is ready the student sprints towards the other line, puts either foot over it and then turns and runs back to the start line. He places either foot over it (fig.30), turns and runs to the far line. Here he turns and sprints back, to cross the start line. The coach starts the stopwatch when either of the

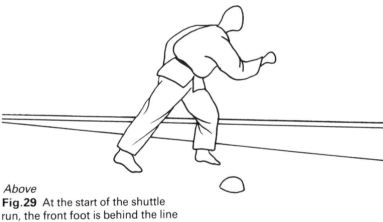

Above
Fig.29 At the start of the shuttle run, the front foot is behind the line

Below
Fig. 30 The shuttle run turn requires one foot to be placed over the line

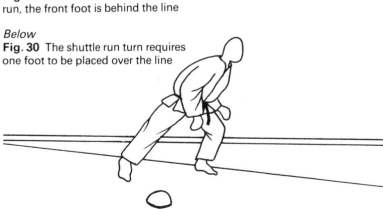

student's feet break contact with the ground at the start, and stops timing him when he crosses the start line at the finish. The student is allowed only one attempt. It is essential that suitable footwear is worn that is non-slip and protects feet and ankles.

This test measures the ability of the student to work maximally for a short period of time. It also gives an idea of his agility in turning and changing direction very quickly, and an assessment of his leg speed.

The Ten-Times-10-Metre (Yard) Shuttle Run

This test is organised in the same way as the Four-Times-10-Metre (Yard) Shuttle Run. This time, however, the student runs 10 times between the two lines. The student is allowed only one attempt. Again, ensure that adequate footwear is worn.

This test measures the ability of a student to work at maximum potential for an intermediate period. The student has to maintain his speed, strength and general ability for a sustained period while fatigue begins to build up.

Sit-ups

The student lies on his back on the floor. A mat is vital to prevent discomfort and possibly injury. He then bends both knees to roughly 90 degrees while a partner firmly anchors his feet. The hands are held at the side of the head. The student sits up until his elbows touch his knees and lies down again (fig 31). The aim is to perform as many sit-ups as possible in

Fig. 31 In sit-ups the knees are bent to 90 degrees. In the movement the elbows are brought up to touch the knees. The feet should be firmly anchored

one minute. Only one attempt is allowed, and the work must be continuous with no rests. When a student has reached one minute or has stopped, the number of sit-ups is recorded.

This test measures the student's ability to work continuously for up to one minute, and shows how fit the abdominal muscles are.

Press-ups

The student assumes the classic press-up position on the floor, ideally with a mat as a precaution against injury. The hands are shoulder-width-apart and the legs, back and shoulders are kept in a straight line. A partner is positioned to put his fist between the mat and the student's chest. The student pushes himself away from the mat (fig. 32) so that both his arms are straight, and then lowers himself back to the mat. On the low part of the press-up he must touch the fist of his partner. The aim is to perform as many press-ups as possible in one minute. As with the sit-ups, work must be continuous, with no rests. Only one attempt is allowed.

This test, like the sit-ups, is a measure of a student's ability to work for up to a minute. It also measures the condition of arms and shoulders.

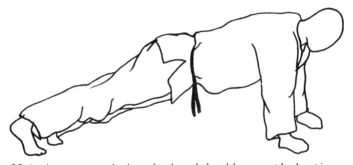

Fig. 32 In the press-up the legs, back and shoulders must be kept in alignment

The Three-Minute Step Test

In this test the student is required to step on and off a bench for three minutes. The bench should be about 30 cm (12 in) high. A step or curb of the same height could be used; gymnasium benches are ideal. It is essential that the same height is used for testing, to make the results valid.

For example, it would be useless to perform one test on a bench 30 cm (12 in) high and the next on a curb of 20 cm (8 in) high. If the coach wants to compare several students, the testing conditions must also be identical. The student is required to step on and off the bench at a rate of 25 steps per minute. The sequence of stepping is:

- both feet together, just in front of the bench (fig.33)
- right foot lifted and placed on the bench top (fig.34)
- left foot lifted and placed alongside the right (fig.35)
- right foot down to starting position
- left foot down to starting position.

A student can also start the sequence with the left foot.

There is a regular, four-beat rhythm to the activity. The coach can call out, 'One—two—three—four' to maintain the rate. Cheap metronomes from music shops can be very useful. For 25 steps per minute, set the metronome at 100 beats per minute to give the four count for each complete step. However if the coach counts the number of steps in a

Left
Fig. 33 The starting position for bench-stepping: stand close to the bench, with both feet together

Right
Fig. 34 The right foot is lifted first, and placed on the bench top

Far right
Fig. 35 The left foot is then brought up beside it

15-second period, he can quickly adjust the rate of stepping. The student is allowed only one attempt at the test.

After stepping for three minutes his pulse is taken immediately on cessation of the work. The count should be taken for a period of 15 seconds and then multiplied by four to give a one-minute pulse count. It is useful if, prior to stepping, a partner finds the student's pulse. Good sites are just above the wrist and below the jaw bone, in line with the ear. When the pulse is taken two fingers should be used. Never use the thumb, because it has its own pulse. Ensure that the person taking the pulse does not become too enthusiastic and press too hard! Any extreme pressure will stop the flow of blood and could be very dangerous.

This test measures the ability of the student to work sub-maximally for up to 3 minutes. This is quite a useful time period, as many competitive styles have 'bouts' lasting two to three minutes. It is also a good indicator of general endurance.

The Five-Minute Step Test

This test is basically the same as the Three-Minute Step Test, but its stepping period is five minutes. The rate of stepping is also different in this case: 30 steps per minute. The metronome should be set at 120 beats. Once again the coach will be able to judge the rate of stepping.

The pulse is taken for 15 seconds and then multiplied by four to give a minute count. However, it is not taken until *one minute after* the cessation of stepping. This test measures the ability of a student to work sub-maximally for periods of up to five minutes. By also showing how quickly the heart rate falls after exercise, it is a measure of recovery.

Left
Fig. 36 The starting position for hamstring flexibility is on a bench with the feet together

Right
Fig. 37 Keeping the legs straight, reach down as far below the bench as possible

Hamstring flexibility

The student stands on a bench (fig.36). One used for stepping is ideal. Keeping both feet together and the legs straight, the student bends down to touch his toes or reach below the level of the bench (fig.37). The hands should be kept side by side and the effort must be maintained for three seconds (fig.38). No bouncing is allowed because it is injurious. Three attempts are permitted and the best effort is recorded. Any reading where the student reaches below the level of his feet should be marked + . If the reading is above the feet it should be indicated with − .

This test measures hamstring and lower back mobility, an essential element of many martial arts techniques.

Hip mobility

The coach will need to obtain two simple pieces of equipment for this test. A pair of blackboard dividers or hinged rulers are required, plus a protractor.

The student sits on the floor and, keeping his legs straight, moves them as far apart as possible. The dividers are placed so that they run down the inside of each leg, with the hinge as close into the crutch as

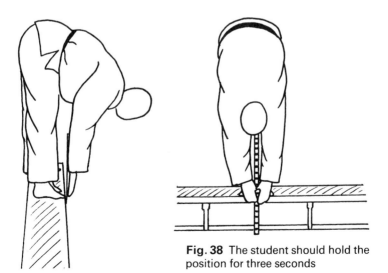

Fig. 38 The student should hold the position for three seconds

possible (fig. 39). Using the protractor, read off the angle produced. Make sure you read the outside of the dividers, the part in contact with the legs (fig. 40).

This test measures the student's ability to move his thighs apart in the lateral plane, an essential aspect of many martial arts techniques.

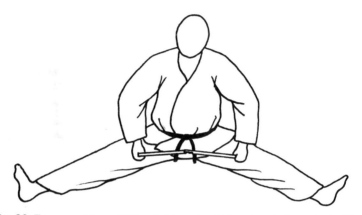

Fig. 39 To assess hip mobility, dividers should be placed along the inside of each leg

Fig. 40 Using a protractor, read off the angle

Turn and Reach

A line is drawn on the floor at right-angles to a wall. It is then extended up the wall to shoulder height. The student stands approximately 60 cm (24 in) away from the wall, with his left side to it and his toes just touching the line (fig.41). He then turns his right arm clockwise to touch the wall, continuing to turn it as far round as possible (fig.42). The feet should be kept in place and not allowed to pivot. The distance that the student can reach beyond the line is measured and indicated with +. If the distance is not as far as the line it should be indicated by −. The student has three attempts and the best effort is recorded.

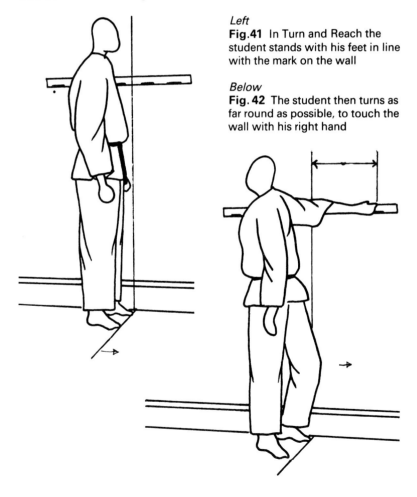

Left
Fig.41 In Turn and Reach the student stands with his feet in line with the mark on the wall

Below
Fig. 42 The student then turns as far round as possible, to touch the wall with his right hand

The coach may wish students to attempt this test with their right side to the wall, turning in an anti-clockwise direction to touch the wall. Once again it will measure the imbalance between the two.

13

The fitness decathlon

For ease of use individual scoring tables in this chapter are arranged into one comprehensive chart. The various activities have been abbreviated as follows:

VJ = Vertical Jump
4*10 = Four-Times-10-Metre Shuttle Run
10*10 = Ten-Times-10-Metre Shuttle Run
SU = Sit-Ups
PU = Press-Ups
3MIN = Three-Minute Step Test
5MIN = Five-Minute Step Test
HAM = Hamstring Flexibility Test
HIP = Hip Mobility Test
TURN = Turn and Reach Test.

This style of presentation makes for easier use and allows one test to be compared with another. If all or several tests are applied to a student, a fitness profile will be produced.

The tests

The tests were devised to be comparable. There should therefore be uniformity in the scores achieved by students in the various tests, plus or minus up to ten points. Any obvious weakness or strength can be identified and training regimes modified accordingly.

The scores in all the tests are designed to be attainable by the 'all-round' martial artist, not just by specialists in a particular style. For example, in Thai Boxing developing tremendous hip mobility is regarded as a level of commitment. If the scores for hip mobility were based on Thai Boxers, very few other styles would score highly. If 'specialists' are tested using these tables, they may well exceed 100 points.

It is useful to apply the following 'correcting factors' when sportsmen (denoted by ($\male$)) and women (denoted by ($\female$)) score over 100 points. For each performance over 100:

Vertical Jump: 1 cm = 1 point

Four-Times-10-Metre Shuttle Run: 0.05 second = 1 point

Ten-Times-10-Metre Shuttle Run: 0.10 second = 1 point

Sit-ups: 1 Sit-Up = 1 point

Press-ups: 1 Press-Up = 1 point

Three-Minute Step Test: for each heartbeat less than 100 ($\male$)/110 ($\female$) score 1 extra point

Five-Minute Step Test: for each heartbeat less than 70 ($\male$)/80 ($\female$) score 1 extra point

Hamstring Flexibility Test: 0.5 cm = 1 point

Hip Mobility: 1.5 Degrees = 1 point

Turn and Reach Test: 2 cm = 1 point.

Using the tables

Once a coach or student has a result from any of the tests he has to convert it into a points score. This is a relatively easy procedure, common for all the tests. For example, a student records a distance of 74 cm or 0.74 m, in the vertical jump. Find the column title VJ, and go down the row of figures until you find 0.74. Then follow the line along to the points column which indicates a score of 74 points. He then scores + 17 cm in the hamstring flexibility test which indicates a score of 84 points.

On average a woman's heart beats approximately 10 times more per minute than a man's. To allow for this, both step tests give male and female pulse counts. In both the three-minute and the five-minute step test, the left-hand column is for men, the right for women. For example, a female student has just completed the three-minute step test and recorded a pulse of 125. Looking down the right-hand side of the two rows of figures in the 3 MIN column gives a score of 75 points.

Sex and age

These tests enable students to compare their performance with previous assessment sessions. Students can also be compared with one another. This is easy if they are of the same gender, but what if the coach wants to compare all the students equally? It is difficult, but as a mathematical exercise this can be done. There are correcting factors for males and females in the step tests, and the coach could apply other correcting factors. If one looks at comparable distance events, for example in athletics and swimming, women run and swim approximately 10% slower than men. The same difference holds for strength, speed, stamina but not suppleness. It is therefore possible to add 10 more points to a female's score, other than for the step tests, to allow it to be compared with a similar male score.

It is also possible to compare, very crudely, the scores of, say, a 15-year-old with those of a 55-year-old. One point per year should be allowed for students over the age of 40. For example, a 15-year-old male performs a vertical jump of 45 cm (18 in), which gives a score of 45 points. A 55-year-old male achieves a jump of 35 cm (14 in) in the same test, which gives a score of 35. Allowing one point per year over the age of 40, 15 points must be added to the mature student's score, making a comparable score of 50 points. The conscientious coach who enjoys maths can allow for both age and sex differences in all of the tests, enabling him to compare the performance of all his students. This task, though daunting, is possible.

The tests have been designed for students to monitor personal progress. However, they can be used in a variety of other ways. Students of different ages and sexes can be compared with one another—the tests can be used as competitions in their own right. How the tests are administered is up to the coach. It takes approximately one hour to test 30 students in all the activities. The coach might want to select a different test each month. He must use these tests, or others, as a formal part of his work programme. Which tests he uses and how he implements them will be up to his professional judgement, which must be respected. Only the coach can have an overall picture of the training programme and what it intends to achieve for his martial art students.

The Fitness Decathlon

PTS	VJ	4×10	10×10	SU	PU
100	1.00	8.00	20.00	80	80
99	0.99	8.05	20.10	79	79
98	0.98	8.10	20.20	78	78
97	0.97	8.15	20.30	77	77
96	0.96	8.20	20.40	76	76
95	0.95	8.25	20.50	75	75
94	0.94	8.30	20.60	74	74
93	0.93	8.35	20.70	73	73
92	0.92	8.40	20.80	72	72
91	0.91	8.45	20.90	71	71
90	0.90	8.50	21.00	70	70
89	0.89	8.55	21.10	69	69
88	0.88	8.60	21.20	68	68
87	0.87	8.65	21.30	67	67
86	0.86	8.70	21.40	66	66
85	0.85	8.75	21.50	65	65
84	0.84	8.80	21.60	64	64
83	0.83	8.85	21.70	63	63
82	0.82	8.90	21.80	62	62
81	0.81	8.95	21.90	61	61
80	0.80	9.00	22.00	60	60
79	0.79	9.05	22.10	59	59
78	0.78	9.10	22.20	58	58
77	0.77	9.15	22.30	57	57
76	0.76	9.20	22.40	56	56
75	0.75	9.25	22.50	55	55
74	0.74	9.30	22.60	54	54
73	0.73	9.35	22.70	53	53
72	0.72	9.40	22.80	52	52
71	0.71	9.45	22.90	51	51

3MIN	5MIN	HAM	HIP	TURN
100/110	70/80	+25.0	180.0	+1.00
101/111	71/81	+24.5	178.5	+0.98
102/112	72/82	+24.0	177.0	+0.96
103/113	73/83	+23.5	175.5	+0.94
104/114	74/84	+23.0	174.0	+0.92
105/115	75/85	+22.5	172.5	+0.90
106/116	76/86	+22.0	171.0	+0.88
107/117	77/87	+21.5	169.5	+0.86
107/118	78/88	+21.0	168.0	+0.84
109/119	79/89	+20.5	166.5	+0.82
110/120	80/90	+20.0	165.0	+0.80
111/121	81/91	+19.5	163.5	+0.78
112/122	82/92	+19.0	162.0	+0.76
113/123	83/93	+18.5	160.5	+0.74
114/124	84/94	+18.0	159.0	+0.72
115/125	85/95	+17.5	157.5	+0.70
116/126	86/96	+17.0	156.0	+0.68
117/127	87/97	+16.5	154.5	+0.66
118/128	88/98	+16.0	153.0	+0.64
119/129	89/99	+15.5	151.5	+0.62
120/130	90/100	+15.0	150.0	+0.60
121/131	91/101	+14.5	148.5	+0.58
122/132	92/102	+14.0	147.0	+0.56
123/133	93/103	+13.5	145.5	+0.54
124/134	94/104	+13.0	144.0	+0.52
125/135	95/105	+12.5	142.5	+0.50
126/136	96/106	+12.0	141.0	+0.48
127/137	97/107	+11.5	139.5	+0.46
128/138	98/108	+11.0	138.0	+0.44
129/139	99/109	+10.5	136.5	+0.42

PTS	VJ	4 × 10	10 × 10	SU	PU
70	0.70	9.50	23.00	50	50
69	0.69	9.55	23.15	49	49
68	0.68	9.60	23.30	48	48
67	0.67	9.65	23.45	47	47
66	0.66	9.70	23.60	46	46
65	0.65	9.75	23.75	45	45
64	0.64	9.80	23.90	44	44
63	0.63	9.85	24.00	43	43
62	0.62	9.90	24.15	42	42
61	0.61	9.95	24.30	41	41
60	0.60	10.00	24.45	40	40
59	0.59	10.05	24.60	39	39
58	0.58	10.10	24.75	38	38
57	0.57	10.15	24.90	37	37
56	0.56	10.20	25.00	36	36
55	0.55	10.25	25.15	35	35
54	0.54	10.30	25.30	34	34
53	0.53	10.35	25.45	33	33
52	0.52	10.40	25.60	32	32
51	0.51	10.45	25.75	31	31
50	0.50	10.50	25.90	30	30
49	0.49	10.55	26.00	29	29
48	0.48	10.60	26.15	28	28
47	0.47	10.65	26.30	27	27
46	0.46	10.70	26.45	26	26
45	0.45	10.75	26.60	25	25
44	0.44	10.80	26.75	24	24
43	0.43	10.85	26.90	23	23
42	0.42	10.90	27.00	22	22
41	0.41	10.95	27.15	21	21

3MIN	5MIN	HAM	HIP	TURN
130/140	100/110	+10.0	135.0	+0.40
131/141	101/111	+09.5	133.5	+0.38
132/142	102/112	+09.0	132.0	+0.36
133/143	103/113	+08.5	130.5	+0.34
134/144	104/114	+08.0	129.0	+0.32
135/145	105/115	+07.5	127.5	+0.30
136/146	106/116	+07.0	126.0	+0.28
137/147	107/117	+06.5	124.5	+0.26
138/148	108/118	+06.0	123.0	+0.24
139/149	109/119	+05.5	121.5	+0.22
140/150	110/120	+05.0	120.0	+0.20
141/151	111/121	+04.5	118.5	+0.18
142/152	112/122	+04.0	117.0	+0.16
143/153	113/123	+03.5	115.5	+0.14
144/154	114/124	+03.0	114.0	+0.12
145/155	115/125	+02.5	112.5	+0.10
146/156	116/126	+02.0	111.0	+0.08
147/157	117/127	+01.5	109.5	+0.06
148/158	118/128	+01.0	108.0	+0.04
149/159	119/129	+00.5	106.5	+0.02
150/160	120/130	+0.00	105.0	0.00
151/161	121/131	−00.5	103.5	−0.02
152/162	122/132	−01.0	102.0	−0.04
153/163	123/133	−01.5	100.5	−0.06
154/164	124/134	−02.0	99.0	−0.08
155/165	125/135	−02.5	97.5	−0.10
156/166	126/136	−03.0	96.0	−0.12
157/167	127/137	−03.5	94.5	−0.14
158/168	128/138	−04.0	93.0	−0.16
159/169	129/139	−04.5	91.5	−0.18

PTS	VJ	4×10	10×10	SU	PU
40	0.40	11.00	27.30	20	20
39	0.39	11.05	27.45	—	—
38	0.38	11.10	27.60	19	19
37	0.37	11.15	27.75	—	—
36	0.36	11.20	27.90	18	18
35	0.35	11.25	28.00	—	—
34	0.34	11.30	28.15	17	17
33	0.33	11.35	28.30	—	—
32	0.32	11.40	28.45	16	16
31	0.31	11.45	28.60	—	—
30	0.30	11.50	28.75	15	15
29	0.29	11.55	29.00	—	—
28	0.28	11.60	29.15	14	14
27	0.27	11.65	29.30	—	—
26	0.26	11.70	29.45	13	13
25	0.25	11.75	29.60	—	—
24	0.24	11.80	29.75	12	12
23	0.23	11.85	29.90	—	—
22	0.22	11.90	30.00	11	11
21	0.21	11.95	30.15	—	—
20	0.20	12.00	30.30	10	10
19	0.19	12.05	30.45	—	—
18	0.18	12.10	30.60	09	09
17	0.17	12.15	30.75	—	—
16	0.16	12.20	30.90	08	08
15	0.15	12.25	31.00	—	—
14	0.14	12.30	31.15	07	07
13	0.13	12.35	31.30	—	—
12	0.12	12.40	31.45	06	06
11	0.11	12.45	31.60	—	—

3MIN	5MIN	HAM	HIP	TURN
160/170	130/140	−05.0	90.0	−0.20
161/171	131/141	−05.5	88.5	−0.22
162/172	132/142	−06.0	87.0	−0.24
163/173	133/143	−06.5	85.5	−0.26
164/174	134/144	−07.0	84.0	−0.28
165/175	135/145	−07.5	82.5	−0.30
166/176	136/146	−08.0	81.0	−0.32
167/177	137/147	−08.5	79.5	−0.34
168/178	138/148	−09.0	78.0	−0.36
169/179	139/149	−09.5	76.5	−0.38
170/180	140/150	−10.0	75.0	−0.40
171/181	141/151	−10.5	73.5	−0.42
172/182	142/152	−11.0	72.0	−0.44
173/183	143/153	−11.5	70.5	−0.46
174/184	144/154	−12.0	69.0	−0.48
175/185	145/155	−12.5	67.5	−0.50
176/186	146/156	−13.0	66.0	−0.52
177/187	147/157	−13.5	64.5	−0.54
178/188	148/158	−14.0	63.0	−0.56
179/189	149/159	−14.5	61.5	−0.58
180/190	150/160	−15.0	60.0	−0.60
181/191	151/161	−15.5	58.5	−0.62
182/192	152/162	−16.0	57.0	−0.64
183/193	153/163	−16.5	55.5	−0.66
184/194	154/164	−17.0	54.0	−0.68
185/195	155/165	−17.5	52.5	−0.70
186/196	156/166	−18.0	51.0	−0.72
187/197	157/167	−18.5	49.5	−0.74
188/198	158/168	−19.0	48.0	−0.76
189/199	159/169	−19.5	46.5	−0.78

PTS	VJ	4 × 10	10 × 10	SU	PU
10	0.10	12.50	31.75	05	05
09	0.09	12.55	31.90	—	—
08	0.08	12.60	32.00	04	04
07	0.07	12.65	32.15	—	—
06	0.06	12.70	32.30	03	03
05	0.05	12.75	32.45	—	—
04	0.04	12.80	32.60	02	02
03	0.03	12.85	32.75	—	—
02	0.02	12.90	32.90	01	01
01	0.01	12.95	33.00	—	—
00	0.00	13.00	33.15	—	—

3MIN	5MIN	HAM	HIP	TURN
190/200	160/170	− 20.0	45.0	− 0.80
191/201	161/171	− 20.5	43.5	− 0.82
192/202	162/172	− 21.0	42.0	− 0.84
193/203	163/173	− 21.5	40.5	− 0.86
194/204	164/174	− 22.0	39.0	− 0.88
195/205	165/175	− 22.5	37.5	− 0.90
196/206	166/176	− 23.0	36.0	− 0.92
197/207	167/177	− 23.5	34.5	− 0.94
198/208	168/178	− 24.0	33.0	− 0.96
199/209	169/179	− 24.5	31.5	− 0.98
200/210	170/180	− 25.0	30.0	− 1.00

Other martial arts books available from A & C Black

Applied Tai Chi Chuan by Nigel Sutton
Elite Karate Techniques by David Mitchell
Health and Fitness in the Martial Arts
    by Dr James Canney
Injury-free Karate by Paul Perry
Jiu Jitsu by Professor Robert Clark
Judo Games by Geof Gleeson
Judo Inside Out by Geof Gleeson
Junior Martial Arts by Tony Gummerson
The Martial Arts Coaching Manual
    by David Mitchell
Martial Arts Injuries by Dr James Canney
Mobility Training for the Martial Arts
    by Tony Gummerson
Okinawan Karate by Mark Bishop
The Police Self-Defence Handbook by Brian Eustace
Self Defence for All by Fay Goodman
Skilful Karate by Greg McLatchie
Strength Training for the Martial Arts
    by Tony Gummerson
Teaching Martial Arts by Tony Gummerson
Winning Karate Competition by David Mitchell
Yang Tai Chi Chuan by John Hine

Index